Setting Up a New Library
and Information Service

LIMERICK CITY LIBRARY

D0784394

CHANDOS
INFORMATION PROFESSIONAL SERIES

Chandos' new series of books are aimed at the busy information professional. They have been specially commissioned to provide the reader with an authoritative view of current thinking. They are designed to provide easy-to-read and (most importantly) practical coverage of topics that are of interest to librarians and other information professionals. If you would like a full listing of current and forthcoming titles, please visit our web site **www.library-chandospublishing.com** or contact Hannah Grace-Williams on email info@chandospublishing.com or telephone number +44 (0) 1865 884447.

New authors: we are always pleased to receive ideas for new titles; if you would like to write a book for Chandos, please contact Dr Glyn Jones on email gjones@chandospublishing.com or telephone number +44 (0) 1865 884447.

Bulk orders: some organisations buy a number of copies of our books. If you are interested in doing this, we would be pleased to discuss a discount. Please contact Hannah Grace-Williams on email info@chandospublishing.com or telephone number +44 (0) 1865 884447.

Setting Up a New Library and Information Service

KIRBY PORTER

Chandos Publishing

Oxford · England · New Hampshire · USA

Chandos Publishing (Oxford) Limited
Chandos House
5 & 6 Steadys Lane
Stanton Harcourt
Oxford OX29 5RL
UK
Tel: +44 (0) 1865 884447 Fax: +44 (0) 1865 884448
Email: info@chandospublishing.com
www.library-chandospublishing.com

Chandos Publishing USA
3 Front Street, Suite 331
PO Box 338
Rollinsford, NH 03869
USA
Tel: 603 749 9171 Fax: 603 749 6155
Email: BizBks@aol.com

First published in Great Britain in 2003

ISBN:
1 84334 053 4 (paperback)
1 84334 054 2 (hardback)

© K. Porter, 2003

British Library Cataloguing-in-Publication Data.
A catalogue record for this book is available from the British Library.

The Publishers make no representation, express or implied, with regard to the accuracy of the information contained in this publication and cannot accept any legal responsibility or liability for any errors or omissions.

The material contained in this publication constitutes general guidelines only and does not represent to be advice on any particular matter. No reader or purchaser should act on the basis of material contained in this publication without first taking professional advice appropriate to their particular circumstances.

Typeset by Monolith – www.monolith.uk.com
Printed in the UK by 4Edge Limited - www.4edge.co.uk

Contents

Introduction   ix

About the author   xi

1   **Why organisations need library and information services**   1

   Why information is important   2

   Why information needs to be managed properly   3

   How you can help   5

2   **First steps to getting started**   9

   Preparation   9

   Finding out about your organisation's information assets   11

   Telling your organisation what you are doing   13

   Finding out how your organisation uses information   16

3   **The importance of customers in the planning and
   development of the new service**   21

   Meeting user demands   22

   Overview of user needs   25

   Summary   28

4   **Managing access to your information – classification**   31

   Preliminary steps   31

   Classification   33

   What a classification scheme looks like   36

   Choosing a classification scheme   40

   General classification schemes   42

Specialist classification schemes   47

How to classify your material   50

5 Managing access to your material – cataloguing   53

What is a catalogue?   54

What elements to include in a cataloguing record   57

Anglo-American Cataloguing Rules   62

Computerised cataloguing systems   66

6 Providing additional material for your users – the art of
stock selection   71

Library budgets   73

Acquisition policy/collection development policy   76

Stock selection   79

The Internet   91

7 Planning further service development   99

What is planning?   99

Service development   104

Circulation   105

Enquiry services   107

Inter-library loans   110

Current awareness   111

Training   113

Journal circulation   114

8 Measuring the performance of the library service   117

The reasons why measuring performance is important   118

Inputs, outputs and outcomes   123

Developing a system for performance measurement   129

9 Marketing the new service   135

Identifying customers   137

Developing a marketing strategy   140

Communicating the message 143

A few last words on marketing 146

10 Conclusion **149**

Appendices

A Useful reference publications 153

B Copyright 157

Index *163*

Introduction

This book is intended as a guide for those people who have been charged with starting up a library or information service in their place of work or who have been asked to consider how such a service could operate. It is primarily for those with little or no prior knowledge of librarianship or acquaintance with the information retrieval skills that are the stock in trade of librarians and who will need guidance on how to start and on the sorts of issues that are involved. It is assumed that they will generally be working on their own with a series of other tasks and responsibilities to perform. Its main purpose is to try to make sense of what can seem to be an almost overwhelming task and to set out in simple terms a step-by-step approach to the problem with easy-to-follow guidelines.

The book will also examine why despite, or perhaps even because of, the growing reliance on information held in electronic format, organisations are only beginning to realise just how important the information they hold is – whether it is produced internally or acquired from external sources – and the important part a properly run library and information service can play in the development of their business. It will also examine how the skills and practice of library professionals can be adapted to provide solutions to the wider problems that issues of information management raise in this context.

The book is intended as a practical guide to the steps that will need to be taken in order to make a success of the venture, the type of people who will normally be encountered and the procedures that will have to be adopted. As such, the book will cover the whole process of creating a library and information service from beginning to end and will be based on an approach that the author has used in practice in a variety of situations in creating a number of new library and information services.

Starting a library and information service in an organisation that has never had one before is both an interesting and challenging venture. It involves hard work and is a long and gruelling process. Yet the rewards can be substantial too. As the library takes shape and begins to offer a professional service, the amazement of customers at the ease with which you can find information that they could never find before, or never knew that the organisation had in the first place, is reward enough for all the hard work and planning that has been undertaken during the project.

While the main emphasis of the book is directed towards those without the basic professional skills of a librarian it should also be of value to both students and those just beginning their professional careers.

Although intended to be read as a whole, each individual chapter can be considered as a useful introduction to the subjects covered. A list of further reading is also included at the end of each chapter for those who wish to explore the various subjects in more depth.

About the author

Kirby Porter was born in Belfast and educated at Queen's University and the University of London. He studied librarianship at the North London Polytechnic School of Librarianship and the University of Wales, Aberystwyth. He was formerly Principal Librarian and Deputy Head of Service with the London Borough of Haringey Community Information Service and is currently Head of the Government Library Service in Northern Ireland and responsible for library services to the Northern Ireland Assembly.

The author can be contacted at:

kirby.porter@dfpni.gov.uk   or
kirby.porter@niassembly.gov.uk

Why organisations need library and information services

It is now a commonplace to state that the majority of businesses and organisations in today's marketplace are dependent on information in its many varieties and guises to such an extent that without access to the right information at the right time they cannot function effectively. The services they deliver to customers, whether internal or external, depends on how well the organisation can create, use and store information to make decisions and thereby act in pursuit of basic business objectives. This information may be created internally or acquired from external sources but wherever it originates it has a value, and often a value which is more than the sums involved in acquiring and storing it. This value can only be realised if the information can be found when needed and used appropriately.

As W.J. Martin put it in *The Global Information Society*:

> The uses to which information is put are quite literally countless, hence the power of those metaphors which link the human and the social organisms in describing information as *the lifeblood of society*. Without an interrupted flow of this vital resource, society as we know it would quickly run into difficulties, with business and

industry, education, leisure, travel and communications, national and international affairs all vulnerable to disruption.[1]

This is what it means to live in what is often called the Information Age or the Information Society.

Why information is important

The achievement of business priorities ultimately depends on the information infrastructure available and poor information management threatens the successful accomplishment of business processes. In order to survive, organisations need staff that are aware of the value of information and understand the mechanisms by which it can be created, stored and accessed. The value of a library and information service at the heart of an organisation and the skills and knowledge of the staff who work there lies in the fact that it creates an information infrastructure that can properly manage the information assets owned by the organisation – in order to make them available to all staff at precisely the time they are needed in a cost-effective way by reducing duplication and unnecessary spending. By classifying and arranging this material in a systematic way so that similar information is held together, staff in the library and information service enable the information to be retrieved quickly and efficiently. In addition, through their knowledge of other libraries and their information holdings they can develop cooperative networks which allow organisations to gain access to information that they do not have themselves and which it would not be practical to purchase in all circumstances.

The majority of organisations have already made a substantial investment in information, through the purchase of books, journals, newspapers, reports and access to information on CD-Rom and online databases, even though this may not be immediately apparent if there is no single point for consolidating these purchases. While considerable organisation goes into the management of other resources such as staff, buildings and equipment, and finance, it has not always been generally recognised how valuable information is as an asset and that it needs to be managed, protected and exploited at least as robustly as those other assets. The role of a library and information service within this context is to put in place those processes which will enable information to be managed properly, in all probability for the first time.

Why information needs to be managed properly

This is important because if these information assets are not being managed properly it will lead directly to a number of problems for the organisation which otherwise could have been avoided. It will lead to disruptions in the information chain so that any, or all, of the following situations may occur:

- Information will not always be available to those that need it when they need it.

- Information may be provided in the wrong format or in a format which does not address the particular needs of users.

- Key activities and decisions that the organisation needs to take may be based on inadequate information or information that is out of date.

- Information that already exists within an organisation may not be shared when appropriate, with additional expenditure incurred in supplying additional copies of information the organisation already holds.

- Information may be retained long after it remains useful so that storage costs are incurred unnecessarily.

Taken together this means that from an asset management perspective, poorly managed information has the potential to incur significant costs for an organisation. This is especially the case in a situation where no one has been given a particular responsibility for ensuring that the necessary management takes place or do not have the necessary skills in order to exercise that responsibility effectively or efficiently. This will inevitably lead to time being wasted or not spent productively by staff who otherwise have other things to do and many other responsibilities. Examples of such wasted time will include numbers of people being involved unnecessarily in:

- searching for information which may or may not be within the organisation and which no one knows how to locate;

- trying to source information which the organisation needs for particular purposes but which it does not have and without anyone really knowing where it can be found;

- checking the accuracy of information once located because no one is certain about the reliability of the source;
- updating information that is out of date;
- trying to understand poorly presented information or transferring it from one context to another, or one format to another;
- understanding the complexity of information held in a number of distinct databases.

As a result of these problems it has been estimated that the amount of time wasted by the average knowledge worker on document-related tasks will increase to between 30 and 40 per cent of their time by 2003.[2]

How you can help

This is an alarming thought. And yet this should not be the case. The very skills that are needed in this situation, the skills needed to manage information properly, the skills of information retrieval, cataloguing, classifying and indexing, are not new but are the stock in trade that librarians have been developing over a great many years. Yet many librarians have been slow to realise the potential that the new situation has for them. Information is important as never before and the need to manage it properly is essential for business survival. As Pantry and Griffith say in their book, *Becoming a Successful Intrapreneur*:

> Management gurus realized that one group of professionals knew all along what needed to be done –

and they named this group. They were the librarians – who always were the true information professionals. Senior managers read the management literature and realized the importance of the resources they already employed. Communities struggling to make sense of the new means of electronic communications came to realize that their libraries could be not only a useful meeting place on winter evenings but also the centre for support in dealing with the new information age.[3]

While this may overstate the case for the wide acceptance of librarians as the means to solve all the problems of information management, it does indicate that more and more often organisations are beginning to turn to librarians to do just that. It also means that you will be able to use these arguments yourself in putting your case for why your organisation should start a new library and information service and for getting your colleagues to support the case.

What exactly these skills are and how they can be used to advantage in setting up a new library and information service will be examined in the following chapters.

Notes

1. William J. Martin (1996) *The Global Information Society.* Aslib/Gower, p. 18.
2. Gartner Research Note SPA-11-9200, 2000.
3. Sheila Pantry and Peter Griffiths (1998) *Becoming a Successful Intrapreneur.* Library Association Publishing, p. ix.

Further reading

Best, David P. (1995) *The Fourth Resource: Information and Its Management*. Aslib/Gower.

Boon, J.A. (1992) 'Information and development: some reasons for failures', *Information Society*, 8, pp. 227–41.

Cronin, Blaise and Davenport, Elisabeth (1991) *Elements of Information Management*. Scarecrow Press.

Wiggins, Bob (2000) *Effective Document Management: Unlocking Corporate Knowledge*. Ashgate.

2

First steps to getting started

In this chapter we will examine how to begin the process of starting up a new library and information service by detailing the first steps that need to be taken. It is assumed that this is a task that you have been given and that there is some measure of support within your organisation for the task ahead: that someone in authority has recognised the need for such a service and thought that you were the one ideally suited to carry it out. This, of course, may not be the case. It might be that you were the one who saw that something needed to be done and have decided that you were going to do it because no one else was going to volunteer in your place.

Preparation

In either case it may be expected that you will be carrying out the work on your own or with the help of a small number of other members of staff. What you need to remember is that the task that you are about to undertake is a time-consuming one and that the resources needed to make a success of it may be substantial, depending on the size of the organisation, the nature of the service you wish to offer and the number of potential customers for that service. You do not have to do everything that is detailed in the chapters that follow or do them in precisely the ways indicated. At best the information given is only a guide to what could be done if the resources were available and you had sufficient time in which to do them. As the process evolves you will be able to consolidate what you have already achieved and be able to plan for the next stage. If this requires additional resources then be prepared to work out in advance what they will be and ask for them in good time. There is no point in starting off in a flurry of optimism and good intentions only for your optimism to disappear when you realise that you will not be able to deliver what you have promised. It is better to achieve what might seem like small improvements than to raise unrealistic expectations of what can be done in particular circumstances.

As with any project you will need to discover what other people in your organisation you need to involve at each stage of the process and what you need to do to get and, more importantly, keep their support. This can be done either informally through direct contact with individuals or more formally through a project board of representatives. This will depend on what works best for your organisation, on how colleagues are used to working and on what makes them most comfortable. You can always try both approaches or change from one to the other as the project develops. In either situation you will need to determine what benefits the new service will bring to your organisation, how it will improve overall business performance and how to bring these benefits to the attention of the people who can get things done. Again, as with other projects, you need to begin at the beginning by finding out about your organisation and the information that it already holds.

Finding out about your organisation's information assets

From the preceding chapter we learnt that the majority of organisations in advanced economies are information based. That is they are dependent on information in order to carry out the various functions that are associated with them as an organisation. This means that they are likely to have already built up substantial information resources which they have collected from time to time in order to meet some immediate information need. This will be in the form of collections of:

- books – either relating to the business of the organisation itself or to the management of organisations in general;

- reports – both internally and externally produced;

- magazines and journals – again relating to the business of the organisation itself or to the management of organisations in general;

- newspapers – national, local or even international;

- legislation – affecting the operation of the organisation or the legal framework in which it operates;

- information held in various electronic formats covering areas similar to the information held in printed format (or, more properly, access to that information).

As there is no existing library and information service this information will not have been held in any central location or managed in any specific way and so will be located in collections which are dispersed throughout the organisation. In order to create a new library and information service it will be essential to discover where these resources are, what has been paid for them, who uses them and for what purposes. The first priority for the new service will be to seek agreement from the users of the material to bring them together in a single collection so that they can form the nucleus of the new service.

In some ways this exercise is similar in nature to the activities which are carried out during an information audit. An information audit – which is about purpose rather than process – seeks to establish what information an organisation needs in order to perform its basic functions and to map that need against the information that it actually has at its disposal in order to establish and fill the gaps in information supply and to deal with other problem areas, such as:

■ the availability of too much information through duplication;

■ the existence of the wrong sort of information held in incompatible formats which is difficult to process and assimilate;

■ the availability of insufficient information.

This is essentially what we are doing here. By gathering together the books and other information which the organisation has already collected we will be able to start the process of creating an interface between that information and the information that the organisation needs to be made available so that it can undertake its various business functions in a correct and proper manner. That interface, once developed, will form the nucleus of the new library and information service.

Although this is a relatively straightforward task, there is no easy way to do it, nor will it always be easy to estimate how long it is likely to take. It will depend on whether you are doing the work on your own, if you have help, the size of the organisation and its location. What it will involve is getting out into the organisation and talking to people about the work they do and the information they have acquired in the course of doing it. It means scouring windowsills and rooting around in old cupboards to see what you can find. It means being prepared to take whatever information comes your way even if it is obvious that it has no value whatsoever. (You can always dispose of it later – but be careful of doing so at this early stage of the project as it will not always be apparent what is or what is not useful. This sort of knowledge will grow the further into the project you get and the more people you talk to.) You will probably be surprised at the results. I always have been.

Telling your organisation what you are doing

Before going to talk to anyone you will need to explain carefully what the purpose of the exercise is and to outline the benefits that good information management with a vibrant library service at its heart will bring to the work they do in terms of easier access to crucial information and a better approach to acquiring information centrally. If you have senior management support, involve them in this initial phase and take every opportunity to inform staff at all levels what you are doing by using every means at your disposal to communicate your message. This will include:

- team briefs
- newsletters
- noticeboards
- information circulars
- e-mails.

The more information that you send out beforehand the easier this will make your initial contacts. For these initial contacts it is best to use the methods that are normally employed in your organisation. Depending on the nature of the organisation this can be done informally or formally but whichever way you chose make sure you do contact them and that it is at a time which is convenient for them. If the project is to succeed then their support will be crucial for you at all stages in the exercise and the better impression you make during this initial contact, the easier you will find it to win their support at a later stage

You should be aware too that not everyone will be pleased to see you and may even see your intervention as a threat. To some, information is power, particularly in organisations where there is no history of information sharing, while others will need to be convinced that anything that they give up will be quickly located for them when they next need it. They may be quite content with the systems they have put in place to meet their immediate needs and see no reason to change.

Obviously, if you have the support of senior management for what you are doing and they have prepared the ground for you in advance by telling staff the purpose of the exercise, some of these problems will not arise, though senior management support is not an absolute guarantee of success. Where you do meet resistance (and some resistance is almost inevitable) you will need to be patient, explain the advantages that the new service will bring to users as individuals, be prepared to listen to what they see as the disadvantages to them and be prepared to be flexible and innovative in your approach. You need to build the service around the needs of users and not expect them to have to adapt to the needs of the service. By talking to them and by listening to what they have to say you will begin to understand the limits of what can be achieved at the beginning of the project. Until staff see the benefits of what you are attempting in terms of how it will affect them and the practical benefits that it will bring, you cannot allow yourself to be disappointed if they are no more than lukewarm at this stage (or even downright hostile). You will need to win their trust and you can only do this through the results you achieve once the new service is operating properly.

One of the benefits of meeting people at this early stage of the project is that you will be developing a range of contacts that can be used later to improve and refine the emerging service. You will have gained a first-hand knowledge of what people in the organisation actually do and start to have an understanding of the information sources that support the various business processes. You will learn the depth of support the move to create a library and information service has among staff in general, what they imagine it can do to help them and how they see it operating over time. With this information you will be able to determine how and in what ways you can involve them in further planning and in taking decisions about how the information sources will be arranged and made available to them as users.

Finding out how your organisation uses information

In the process of gathering the existing information resources together you will have a unique opportunity to find out more about how the organisation used its information in the past and how it could do so more efficiently in the future. The detailed information that you need here relates to what has been purchased in the past and what happened to it afterwards. In particular you will need to find out at this stage:

- what stock of books and other information resources are held by the organisation;
- where they are located and in what formats they are held;
- who was responsible for their acquisition;
- how much they cost and how they were acquired;
- who manages and maintains the collections;
- who has access to the material and who controls that access;
- how the access is provided;
- how effective the use of the information resources is in supporting business needs;
- if acquisition fulfilled the purchase that was intended;
- how efficient the systems are in terms of the effort required to use and maintain them;

- what processes are in place when information goes missing or is not there in the first place;
- what level of support there is for the project among staff.

Before asking these questions it is impossible to tell what sort of information you will get and how much of it will be useful. It will depend on whether or not there is any sort of mechanism in place for managing the material and how much is actually acquired. Do not be surprised, however, to find out that once the material is purchased then there is no actual management involved and that the only person who can access anything is the person who ordered it in the first place. If you do get any useful information at this point, some of it will be used immediately while the rest will form part of the background information that will inform further stages of the project by outlining the problems that you will need to overcome and the range of services that may be deployed to meet the expectations that staff have for the new service.

Of course there are certain things that you must do before going out into the organisation to talk to people. You must:

- ensure that you have a room equipped with shelving that is big enough to house the material that you will be gathering;
- ensure that adequate publicity has been given to the project which explains what you are hoping to achieve and how it will benefit the organisation;
- ensure that you have enough time to cover all aspects of this phase of the project, especially if you discover that there is more out there than you originally thought.

Once this part of the project is complete you will not only have a substantial collection of material which will form the nucleus of the new library and information service but also have gained a valuable insight into what the organisation does and how it handles information. In particular you will have gained:

- an understanding of how your organisation works;
- a knowledge of the information sources currently available to the organisation, how they are used and by whom;
- who the likely customers of the new service will be and how supportive of the new arrangements they will be;
- an understanding of the problems the organisation has had in the past with the supply of information and customer expectation of how the new service will change this;
- what the priorities of the new service should be.

All of this will help with the next phase of the project which is to arrange your material in a way that will make it accessible for your users. This will be discussed in later chapters but before that it will be necessary to have a closer look at library users in order to position them at the heart of the new service.

Further reading

Bryson, Jo (1998) *Effective Library and Information Centre Management*. Ashgate.

Harrod's Librarians' Glossary and Reference Book: a directory of over 9,600 terms, organisations, projects and acronyms in the areas of information management, library science, publishing and archive management (1999) Ashgate.

Jordan, Peter and Lloyd, Caroline (2002) *Staff Management in Library and Information Work*, 4th edn. Ashgate.

3

The importance of customers in the planning and development of the new service

As indicated in the previous chapter, perhaps the most important aspect of the work that you have just carried out during the initial stages of the information audit is that it will have brought you into contact with staff who need access to information in your organisation and as a result are likely to become users of the new service. This is important because if the service is to have any relevance for your organisation, then you will need to develop the service in ways which will be most helpful to them and which places their needs at the very centre of library planning and development.

A library service is fit for its purpose not because it meets some archetypal professional standard but because it satisfies the demands that users place on it and, as a consequence, can add value to the organisation by meeting those demands in the most effective and efficient ways. Meeting user demand will thus have relevance not only for determining what material is purchased but also for how it is arranged within the library, for how users gain access to it and for the varied ways in which information is used by individuals. The service must be customer-focused in every aspect of its operation or it will simply not survive.

Meeting user demands

In considering the needs of users in this context it is important to develop an understanding of who exactly your users or customers are and how they use or could use the services that you are offering. Some of this information you will already have gained in the work carried out so far but it is worth repeating. Broadly speaking you need to know:

- who your users are and what exactly they do in the organisation;
- what library-type needs they have or are likely to have;
- how they might use the library – whether in person, by telephone, or by proxy;
- what information resources you have to meet these needs; and
- what alternative library sources are available to them.

Knowledge of this will enable you to build up a picture of how to position the library for maximum effect and will determine exactly what the library should do to support the work that users carry out. As has been noted, a lot of this information will have been discovered during the course of the information audit but it is important to remember that just because you have gathered this information once it will always be valid. Things change. Staff are given new responsibilities and hence develop new information needs. They move job. The organisation itself may change the focus of its business or need to respond to new markets, new business opportunities or new initiatives from the government. The nature of information also changes – how it is supplied, how it is accessed, how much it costs – and this too will change how users respond to the library service on offer and what they expect the library to do. The growth of the Internet, for example, and the way it orders information has had a profound effect on the way libraries operate – and not only in the more obvious ways. Because of this the library cannot afford to remain static and even as you begin to develop library services to meet current responsibilities and current needs you should also be considering how you can build the required degree of flexibility into your systems, so that you can respond quickly when these responsibilities and needs change. In everything you do you must ensure that whatever decisions are taken do not bind you into a way of doing things that cannot be easily changed or amended once taken. You job is to be able to respond to user need, whatever it may be, because if you do not your users will simply go elsewhere.

Remember, too, that users are individuals and that your job will be to tailor the service, within the constraints of time and money, to meet the needs of those individual users. Not everyone reacts in the same way and it is important to consider how this will effect what you do. You need to take note of the following:

- The individuals that you meet will probably have more than one different aspect to their job and each of these roles will have a different information requirement attached to it: with the relative importance of these functions also changing over time.

- They will come from a wide range of backgrounds with differing experiences of library and information services and differing expectations of how such services should operate and what they want from them.

- They are not predictable in their needs or in the levels of experience and understanding they have of the information which is available to meet those needs.

- They are not predictable in the use to which they will put the information once found.

- They have a choice over whether or not to get information in the first place and in the level of detail they require.

- They have a choice over whether to get the information from your library service or from some other source or sources that they may also have.

This last element is crucial: while some will welcome the librarian's initiative in informing them of the nature and extent of the services they are offering by bringing to their notice recent publications in fields they are interested in, for example, others will see it as an intrusion which actually causes them work rather than as a time-saving service. Your job will be to find the extent to which individuals want you to be actively involved in working with them and to provide a service that operates on many levels and has more than just a single point of engagement.

While this aspect of individual engagement and its importance for service development cannot be stressed too strongly it is still possible, nevertheless, to generalise to a certain extent on the outline nature of information need which can be used to form the basis of the new service being developed. This too is important for while users are individuals with individual needs, they do share certain characteristics which will enable you to define and describe the parameters for a basic service. This can then be further refined to meet the more complex needs of particular groups of users and individuals within these groups.

Overview of user needs

In this general sense information needs can be grouped together under a number of common headings which in turn indicate the sort of material that the library and information service will have to collect in order to meet these needs. By considering general needs in this way you can then assess them against the material you have already collected and identify the immediate gaps that you have by assessing the various strengths and weaknesses of your collection that will become apparent. In this general scheme individuals and organisations can be said to have a number of information needs which can be analysed in the following ways.

1. A need for information which is current and up to date and a way of being made aware of it

In the current age the need to know is paramount – individuals and organisations need to keep up to date, they want to read the latest books and have access to the latest reports which affect the work they do. They need to know the current news. They need to know about how changes in legislation will impact on how their organisation operates. They need to know about markets and their competitors and the latest innovations in product development and in how to do business. A lot of this information will relate directly to the nature of the organisation itself and should be well represented in the material that you have already collected. The task of the new library service will be to make sure that access to this information is given to everyone who needs it in the organisation and to develop ways of alerting staff to new information as it arises.

2. A need for information specific to the functions that they carry out through research and related activities

This is information which is directly related to the jobs individuals perform in their organisation, the essential bulk of material without which it would be impossible for them to function properly or for them to be able to take on new tasks or projects. Again you would expect this to be well represented in your collection as it relates in some ways to the information in (1) above.

3. A need for specific information in response to general enquiries

This is basically factual information and is often described as quick-reference information. While these quick-reference needs are often simple, nevertheless they are likely to be urgent and, more importantly, the type of enquiry that the library and information service will be expected to answer without fuss. They range from how to spell a word or how to find a telephone number to details about train, bus or airplane timetables – or, indeed, about almost anything else at all. Given that your organisation is only developing a library and information service it is unlikely that you will find much if any of this material already in the collection. This is an area that is worth developing, as it will position the library as somewhere for staff to go when seeking answers to questions which otherwise may waste them a lot of time (see Appendix A).

4. A need for information which will help users improve the work they do

Personal development is now an important component of jobs in many organisations, as individuals are required to update their skills on a continuing basis in order to function effectively in the workplace. This can take the form of formal study with set texts and required reading lists but may also relate to less formal study where the information needed is likely to be more wide-ranging and less well stated. Under this heading would come books and other information sources about management, business, administration and finance, training manuals and other items. This will be another area which is likely to have been neglected in a situation where there has been no library to provide this sort of service, and it is one which can be used to extend the range of material that the library holds.

5. General reading needs

This is another less well-stated area but may well be required in order to ensure that sufficient access is provided to those areas of broader knowledge which the library could usefully exploit to create the wider information context in which the work of individuals is exploited.

Summary

The overview of user needs which emerges from the above analysis may be a very general one but it is another useful tool which you can use in order to form the basic shape of how the library should be positioned within your organisation. At this stage you should be equipped with the following information:

- an overview of what information the organisation holds;
- an overview of the specific information customers need in order to undertake the specific functions of their jobs;
- an overview of general information need.

An analysis of this will give a good indication of the sort of services the library will need to develop in order to fully satisfy customer requirements and will suggest the areas in which further work will need to be concentrated during the initial phase of service development. It will also provide the basis which will allow you to develop a framework for organising and arranging the collection in a manner which will best suit the way in which your users think about information. We will look at that in more detail in the next chapter.

Further reading

Calvert, Philip (2003) *Analysing What Your Users Need: A Guide for Librarians and Information Managers*. Facet Publishing.

Lax, Stephen (2001) *Access Denied in the Information Age*. Palgrave.

Lushington, Nolan (2002) *Libraries Designed for Users: A 21st Century Guide*. Neal-Schuman Publishers.

Verlejs, Jana (1988) *Information Seeking: Basing Services on Users' Behaviour*. McFarland & Co.

Whitlack, Jo Bell (1985) *Library Users and Reference Services*. Haworth Press.

4

Managing access to your information – classification

The next stage in the process of creating your new library and information service is to organise the material that you have already collected in order to manage access to it. In broad terms this means arranging the material in such a way that users know what material is available and where in the library it can be found. As you will have collected the material from a variety of sources over the period of time it took to complete the information audit, the collection will be very difficult to manage as it stands. The first step will be to put the material in some sort of order and then to refine this order once you understand the complete nature of the collection.

Preliminary steps

The easiest way to start the process is to organise the material into broad categories and then to analyse the content of each category to see what it is that you actually have. The material that you have received can be divided into:

- journals
- newspapers
- reports

- legislation
- books.

These categories can then be further divided so that journals are organised by title, reports by the names of the organisations they come from, books by a broad classification based on subject, and so on. It must be emphasised that this temporary arrangement should not influence the final arrangement of the material but it will allow you to do several things that will help bring the collection under more proper control. For example:

- it will allow you to check for missing items of particular journals and to see what journals the organisation has taken subscriptions to in the past but has not kept up to date;
- it will allow you to consider books and other material that you have more than one copy of and to discover superseded editions of others and books which are out of date and no longer valuable.

Disposing of material which has no apparent value will make the job of organising the collection that much easier but before you take the step of throwing anything away you should check with your users (usually the person who gave you the material in the first place) whether or not it should be disposed of. Subscriptions to journals may have lapsed simply because no one had got round to renewing them and older material may still have a value to your users. The skill of knowing what to keep and what to throw away is something that you will only learn over time as you come to know your users better and the way in which they use information. By classifying and arranging the material in a proper fashion you will be able to identify patterns of use that will help you gain this knowledge through an understanding of subject usage and the manner and format in which information has been collected in the past.

Once this exercise is complete you will be left with a core collection of material that can now be organised to the standards you devise. In the next section we will examine what classification is and how to choose a classification standard that will help your customers find the information they need.

Classification

The purpose of classification is to arrange the material you have gathered in a systematic way in order to make the retrieval of that material relatively straightforward for users of the service. While material can be classified and arranged into subject order as an end in itself, the fact that librarians use it as a retrieval tool is important as this will determine the scope and nature of the classification scheme used. If you have only ten books in your collection then it hardly matters how they are arranged – retrieval will not be a problem. The greater the amount of material within the library collection and the more diverse needs your users have for this material, the greater the requirement for a more complex classification scheme. If one of your library users, for example, has a specific requirement for information about the legal system in New South Wales and you have many hundreds of legal texts which could potentially hold such information then having them classified simply under the single subject term Law will not be of much use. What you will need is to develop a more sympathetic approach – sympathetic to the needs of the user, that is.

The systematic arrangement of knowledge, or in your case the systematic ordering of books and other material in your collection, will have two important functions as an aid to retrieval in these circumstances:

- it provides for an overview of coverage within the collection on a subject basis;
- it enables information to be retrieved from the collection without the whole collection being searched.

As a result, retrieval will be quicker and more efficient. A classification achieves this by:

- creating a link between the location of an item within the library with the library catalogue by using the classification number as a shelf mark;
- allowing for direct retrieval by browsing – if the subject classification is known then all books in that subject area will be collocated on the library shelves and related subjects are likely to be found nearby.

Depending on the nature and complexity of the collection, either a general or a special classification scheme can be used to arrange the collection by subject. As the name suggests, a general classification scheme is one which is applied to all subjects and thus has a place for any book no matter what the subject area is. A public library would be a good example of an institution using a general classification scheme. On the other hand a library would use a special classification scheme when the collection consists of material where only a limited number of subjects are involved, when a library only contains specialist legal material for example, and the need to be as specific as possible in determining subject areas is required (not just law but legal systems, not just legal systems but Australian legal systems, not just Australian legal systems but legal systems in New South Wales, to use the example above).

In choosing a classification scheme you will need to decide at the outset which of the two approaches best suits your library collection and the needs of your users and whether in choosing how to classify your material you want to devise one of your own or simply adapt an already existing one. In order to make the correct decision you will need to consider:

- the nature of the library collection;
- how your users will use the library – either in person or mediated by library staff;
- how complicated the classification scheme needs to be in order to sufficiently differentiate material so that retrieval will be relatively straightforward;
- how the library will ensure that staff doing the classification are consistent in their approach;
- how important it is to locate material on similar subjects beside one another.

The answers to these questions will give a good indication of the sort of classification scheme that will be needed. It is important to remember too that someone will have to do the classification work and that the availability of staff resources for the task will determine the extent to which it can be carried out successfully. This in turn will affect your decision on whether to develop your own classification scheme or use an existing published one. But more about that later.

What a classification scheme looks like

Before going on to consider questions of particular classification schemes and how they might be used, we need to look at the way they work in a general sense. As stated earlier, a classification scheme is simply a systematically arranged collection of material which allows an individual item from that collection to be retrieved easily. It can be as simple or as complex as you like, depending on the complexity of the collection that must be managed.

However, for any particular scheme to work properly the staff using it must apply the rules for classifying material in a consistent way so that material on the same subject is always placed together and not distributed throughout the collection. To take a simple example – a collection of cutlery all of the same type and variety could be sorted into the simple categories of knives, forks and spoons and stored accordingly. This would make the retrieval of an individual spoon an equally simple task. In a similar way, if you had only 10 books to arrange and each book was on a different subject then by labelling them 1–10 you would have created a classification scheme. If you increased your collection to 26, again with only one book on each subject, then you could label them 1–26, or indeed, A–Z.

However, to take our cutlery analogy a stage further, if our collection expanded to include fish knives, soup spoons, dessert forks, teaspoons, tablespoons, carving knives and any other type of knife, fork or spoon that you can think of, and some were made of stainless steel, some silver, some gold, of different size and shape, and so on then the retrieval of an individual spoon would be accordingly more difficult if we retained our simple classification of knives, forks and spoons.

In the same way, as we add more books to our original 10 then the sort of arrangement envisaged above will start to break down. You may have so many books on a particular broad subject that you will need to subdivide it into its component parts. You may need to place related or similar subjects side by side in order to provide browsing options for your users. New subjects may arise that need to be differentiated from old ones but still need to be related to them nonetheless. A classification scheme to be of any real use in retrieval must be sufficiently flexible to allow for any of these emerging difficulties as the collection grows, without requiring that the whole collection be reclassified over and over again.

In order to achieve this the classification scheme that you choose or devise will need to consist of a number of different components that will allow the scheme to function properly and will provide the necessary framework and rules to ensure consistency of use. Thus any effective classification scheme should consist of the following components:

- schedules – which allow subjects to be listed in a systematic way and which create relationships between various subjects;
- notation – which describes the subjects and their relationships using an alphabetic or numeric code (or a combination of the two);
- an alphabetic index of subjects which allows for easy identification of the subject with the chosen code.

The schedules themselves should be made up in the following way:

- with main subject areas or classes (for example, Science, Technology, Art, ...);
- with subdivisions which properly should only use one characteristic to differentiate them at a time (for example, Science can be subdivided into Biology, Chemistry, Physics).

This will allow complex subject areas to be created and their relationship with other subjects to be maintained in a consistent and coherent way.

This type of approach to classification is called enumerative classification and is an attempt to create a specific place within the scheme for each and every possible subject area. This, however, is a daunting task and most such schemes are necessarily only selective. This method of compiling a classification scheme does bring some problems with it. The schedules can seem repetitive and there will be occasions when a particular book could be placed in more than one position in the scheme. Where, for example, would a book entitled, *The History and Politics of France* be placed in such a scheme? In addition, it is also the case that disciplines do not remain static but are constantly evolving and changing so that new subject fields emerge and others take on distinct new meanings and relationships.

The other general approach to classification is termed *faceted classification*. Faceted classification is a scheme of classification which reflects in its structure the analysis of subjects based on a number of fundamental concepts, principally those of:

- personality
- matter
- energy
- space
- time.

All modern classification schemes are faceted to some degree but in a proper faceted scheme the terms are grouped by conceptual categories and ordered so that they display their generic relations. These categories are used to create the notation for the scheme by combining category numbers in a prescribed way.

It is worth considering the question of notation in a more general sense. Notation is the code that you apply to your material in order to fix its position on the library shelves. Once the classification schedules have been arrived at and the subjects to be included and the order in which they will appear in the schedules have been determined, notation is used to differentiate the subject areas and fix them in relation to one another. This is best explained by looking at how particular schemes use it and we will do this later in the chapter. At this stage it is sufficient to take a note of the following characteristics:

- it should be flexible enough to allow for your subject fields to be expanded if necessary and for new subjects to be included where they will be most useful;

- the notation should be easy to use both for library staff and, more importantly, library users.

Notation is used by library staff to fix the location of the material on shelves and by library users to find the material they want, either directly by reference to notation information found on the library catalogue or indirectly through browsing. This process is aided by the use of an alphabetic index which allows staff and users to fix the notation to individual subjects and brings together the related aspects of a subject which may appear in more than one place in the schedules.

Choosing a classification scheme

While it is perfectly possible to devise your own classification scheme, and this may be the preferred option depending on the nature of the collection involved (the number of books you have and how specialist they are), you should first consider whether you will have the time and the resources to devote to the task of both developing a scheme and then maintaining it. There is always the danger too that the scheme you create will be inadequate as it will be based solely on the books currently in the collection and on the current needs of your users. This is unfortunately very likely to happen when you create a new library and information service and do not yet have all the information about users and their needs necessary for the task. This lack of information may not allow you to take fully into consideration the way in which the collection may grow and the ways in which the information needs of your users will change over time. If the chosen classification and its accompanying notation is not flexible enough you may find that at a later date new material arrives which you cannot fit into your scheme at the appropriate place and as a consequence may need to do the work all over again.

An alternative is to use a classification scheme that has already been devised and is in operation in a variety of established libraries. For example, you may find it advantageous to use the same classification scheme of another library that your users use or that you may be associated with for organisational reasons. While this will not completely guarantee that you will be able to classify every new subject that has to be integrated into your collection it is likely, on balance, that fewer such occasions will arise and that the need for maintenance of the classification scheme will not become overwhelming. There are a number of such schemes either of a general or specialist nature which you could choose, all of which have formidable infrastructures attached for revision and maintenance.

General classification schemes

There are three major general classification schemes in use in libraries:

- the Dewey Decimal Classification Scheme (DDC);
- the Universal Decimal Classification Scheme (UDC) – derived from DDC;
- the Library of Congress Classification Scheme (LCC).

DDC was devised in 1876 by Melvil Dewey, an American college librarian. It introduced a number of new features to the act of classifying in libraries and a number of refinements were developed over time through revision. These features included:

- the use of relative as opposed to fixed location, i.e. books were shelved according to their subject content rather than by the date when they were acquired by the library;
- decimal notation was used as a means of differentiating subject areas based on numbers in the range 000–999;
- decimal subdivision was then used as a means to refine subject areas further and make classifying more precise;
- tables of what Dewey called 'form divisions' were introduced to represent common facets which could be applied to any number (geographical area, historical period).

DDC works by creating a number of main classes as shown below:

000 – Generalities

100 – Philosophy, paranormal phenomena, psychology

200 – Religion

300 – Social sciences

400 – Linguistics

500 – Natural sciences and mathematics

600 – Technology

700 – The arts

800 – Literature

900 – Geography and history

Then, the subject areas are expanded by further subdividing these numbers so that Social sciences in the 300 area, for example, are expanded according to the following pattern:

300 – Social sciences

310 – General statistics

320 – Political science

330 – Economics

340 – Law

350 – Public administration

360 – Social problems and services

370 – Education

380 – Commerce, communication and transportation

390 – Customs, etiquette and folklore

These subdivisions themselves can then be further divided using the same principles so that the more precise classification number is arrived at. For example, '362 – Social welfare problems and services' can be further broken down by using decimal subdivision to create the following array of numbers:

362.1 – physical illness

362.2 – mental and emotional illness

362.3 – mental retardation

362.4 – problems of and services to people with physical disabilities

362.5 – problems of and services to the poor

362.6 – problems of and services to persons in late adulthood

362.7 – problems of and services to young people

362.8 – problems of and services to other groups

362.9 – historical, geographic, persons treatment

and so on.

The full edition of DDC is published and arranged in four volumes:

Volume 1 – Tables

Volume 2 – Schedules 000–599

Volume 3 – Schedules 600–999

Volume 4 – Index

There is also a CD-Rom version of Dewey for Windows. While it is not a perfect classification scheme by any means, it does have a pragmatic robustness that enables it to be used in all but the most specialist libraries. A single-volume abridged edition is published alongside every full edition (published every seven years, the last in 1996) and a further abridgement – DDC for school libraries – is also available.

Library of Congress Classification

As the name suggests this is the classification scheme used in the United States Library of Congress (the main legal deposit library in the USA, their equivalent of the British Library) and was developed when the Library of Congress moved to new premises in 1897. As such it was developed to meet the needs of Congress as they were perceived at that time. Each of the classes was devised separately over time (with class K Law not complete until 1993) and can be used separately. This means that the classification is almost entirely enumerative and as a consequence tends to be repetitive. This also means that the schedules themselves are very bulky. The main classes consist of the following:

A – General works

B – Philosophy, psychology, religion

C – Auxiliary sciences of history

D, E, F, – History

G – Geography and anthropology

H – Social sciences

J – Political science

K – Law

L – Education

M   – Music

N   – Fine arts

P   – Language and literature

Q   – Science

R   – Medicine

S   – Agriculture

T   – Technology

U   – Military science

V   – Naval science

Z   – Bibliography and library science

LCC is then subdivided using the following general method. Taking the class H, Social sciences, we get:

H	Social sciences
HM–HX	Sociology
HV	Social pathology, Social and public welfare, Criminology
HV 6001–9920	Criminology
HV 6254–6773	Special crimes
HV 6435–6492	Offences against public order
HV 6435–6453	Illegal organisations
HV 6441–6453	Outlaws, Brigands, Feuds[1]

This example gives only a flavour of how the scheme proceeds as it is important to remember that it is an enumerative scheme rather than one which is based on general principles. As a result the scheme, and how to apply it, can only be learnt through practice. Rather than be seen as a weakness, however, this is actually one of the scheme's great strengths. Every class, and every subdivision within each class, only exists because at one time subject specialists have seen the need for it and because the same subject specialists have developed the detail of the classes against the specification of an actual collection of material, i.e. the material held within the Library of Congress. Thus it is highly unlikely that you will come across many subjects in your collection that do not have an equivalent subject entry in LCC. Whether you agree with how that subject has been positioned is another matter!

If the main bulk of your own collection falls within one of the classification's main classes then it would be possible, even desirable, to use LCC to classify that material while using a classification scheme of your own devising (or possibly even DDC) to classify the rest of the collection.

Because of the nature of the work of the Library of Congress, new classmarks are created as they are needed (i.e. when new works on subjects not previously classified are deposited in the library). A list of these classmarks is published in the Library's Information Bulletin and the CD-Rom version of the scheme is updated annually. In addition there are a number of other guides and useful publications also available.

Specialist classification schemes

In general terms specialist classification schemes are designed to cover one subject area or to meet the interests or information requirements of particular user groups. This can include:

- classification schemes restricted to conventional subject areas such as law, medicine or music;
- classification schemes designed to cover subject areas in a particular context like local collections;
- classification schemes designed to satisfy the needs of particular users like architects, accountants and so on.

Moys Classification Scheme for law books

This scheme was developed in 1982 by Elizabeth Moys and was originally intended to stand in for the Library of Congress's then unpublished class K law. The scheme incorporates both enumerative number building concepts, i.e. by the use of tables of numbers to expand an already allocated block of numbers (as you would expect based on the Library of Congress classification scheme) and the faceted theory adopted by Dewey with its subject approach.

Because of the difficulty associated with mixing primary and secondary law, Moys approaches its subject classification initially in terms of jurisdiction. The scheme is split into the following sections:

- Primary law
- Secondary law
- Law reference
- Law journals.

The material is then arranged within each of these. So within Primary law, for example, for material that consists of documents that contain the law, namely legislation and law reports based on jurisdiction, English law is broken down in the following way:

KF	Great Britain
KF 20–34	English legislation
KF 51–54	English reports of cases before 1865
KF 55	English authorised law reports after 1865
KF 60	English general law reports
KF 65	English specialised law reports
KF 101–160	Scottish legislation and law reports
KF 201–260	Irish legislation and law reports

Other jurisdictions are handled in a similar fashion.

Within Secondary law, i.e. textbooks and monographs which provide commentary on the primary material, the division is by subject according to the following arrangements:

KA – Jurisprudence

KB – General and comparative law

KC – International law

KD – Religious legal systems

KE – Ancient and medieval law

KL – Legal systems – common law

KM – Public law

KN – Private law

How to classify your material

Once you have chosen your classification scheme, whether it is one of your own devising or an established model, you will then need to apply the scheme in a consistent way to ensure uniformity so that material of a similar nature is held in the same place in the library. In order to do this you will need in the first place to analyse the subject matter of the book or material to hand. This can be done in a number of ways:

- Use the title, subtitle and the contents list at the front of the book to try and determine what the subject of the book is. Sometimes this will be straightforward, for example for a book entitled *Pure Mathematics*, and sometimes misleading, for example *The Bridges of Madison County* is not a book about bridges.

- Use the author's introduction as a way of finding out more about the book.

- Consider who the book is for and where the information about it came from in the first place, from a review or a subject bibliography.

- Look at outside sources like the British National Bibliography to see how they classified the material.

- Make sure to define the subject covered as precisely as possible and then look to your scheme to find the best match possible.

Even when you have done all this it may not be possible to identify a single subject which covers all the aspects of a particular item. In these situations you will need to determine which subject area provides the best fit. This should be done by considering how that item is likely to be viewed by your library users, that is, how are they likely to regard it and where would they expect it to be placed in the collection? Remember too that in a given subject the general expectation is that the more important facet of the subject will be given precedence so that a book about medieval castles is better placed with other books about castles rather than with other books about medieval architecture. In the end, though, you will have to make a judgement based on your knowledge, experience and past practice as there is no definitive right or wrong answer in classification.

Once you have decided on the subject area you then need to check your own catalogue to see how you classified similar subjects on previous occasions. This check is vital if the integrity of the classification scheme and the library catalogue is to be maintained. If it is a new subject area for the library, then you need to check the index and schedules of your classification scheme if you are using a standard one or create a new subject area and number if you have created your own classification scheme. As a final step you can look at the books surrounding the new edition on the library shelves to check that it does not look out of place where you have put it.

Note

1. Example taken from Jennifer Rowley and John Farrow (2000) *Organizing Knowledge: An Introduction to Managing Access to Information*, 3rd edn. Gower, p. 228.

Further reading

Buchanan. B (1979) *Theory of Library Classification*. Bingley.

Foskett, A.C. (1996) *The Subject Approach to Information*, 5th edn. Bingley.

Ganendran, Jacki (2001) *Learn Library of Congress Subject Access*, Workbooks for Learning Cataloguing and Classification Schemes. Scarecrow Press.

Hunter, E.J. (2002) *Classification Made Simple*, 2nd edn. Ashgate.

Langridge, D.W. (1992) *Classification: Its Kinds, Systems, Elements and Applications*. Bowker-Saur.

Marcella, Rita and Maltby, Arthur (2000) *The Future of Classification*. Ashgate.

Mortimer, Mary (2001) *Learn Descriptive Cataloguing*, Workbooks for Learning Cataloguing and Classification Schemes. Scarecrow Press.

Scott, Mona L. (1998) *Dewey Decimal Classification, 21st Edition: A Study Manual and Number Building Guide*. Greenwood Press.

5

Managing access to your information – cataloguing

Now that you have arranged and classified the material in your collection it is possible to create catalogue records for them. Cataloguing has long been considered one of the least interesting aspects of library work and is now not a compulsory element in many librarianship courses. Indeed, it is hardly taught at all any more. This is a pity because it is still important and even in the days of computerised catalogues there is still more to cataloguing than simply following a set of easily defined rules. Some judgement will always be necessary and the benefits that a good catalogue will bring to users are worth the effort of spending some time getting it right.

The main purpose of cataloguing is to describe the contents of your library in such a way that users will be able to determine whether or not an item that they are looking for is contained in the collection. It is well, at this early stage, not to lose sight of this and to keep the user's perspective of what the catalogue is for at the centre of the cataloguing process. How detailed you make the catalogue entries will depend on the resources you can afford to commit to the process and on how your users will use the catalogue that you have created. The most important consideration in this sense is to ensure that any material that you buy for the library is quickly made available to users rather than spending unnecessary months on a cataloguer's desk being processed.

Catalogues are important, however, because of the assistance they give to users in providing them with a means of retrieving the particular items that they want in a systematic way. A good catalogue also brings a known order to the arrangement of the material in the collection and this too can become an aid to retrieval. This means that whatever arrangements you make for cataloguing within your collection, the individual catalogue records should be presented in a clear and logical way so that the underlying structure is easy for users to comprehend. While total consistency may be impossible to achieve in a working situation, every effort should be made to keep any inconsistencies to an absolute minimum. Everyone who is engaged in the cataloguing process should understand the structure of the catalogue and the underlying rules supporting it. Changes to or deviations from either the structure or the rules should only be sanctioned by someone who has been given the authority to make them. Ideally this authority should be invested in a single individual.

What is a catalogue?

A catalogue in this library sense then is simply a list of all the materials in the collection with the catalogue records representing the material arranged for access in an ordered and systematic way. In most libraries nowadays these records are held as a computer database with access to them from Online Public Access Catalogues (OPACs) (this is discussed in more detail later in the chapter) either located within the library or remotely from the user's desktop, although they can just as easily be held as a card catalogue or on microform or even as a printed book. Whatever the format the catalogue remains the same, comprising a number of discrete entries which can be considered as an access point for an item in the collection. Depending on the complexity of the catalogue each item may have only one point of access or a number of them.

In a strict sense the concept of access points relates primarily to a manual catalogue where each access point (author, title, etc.) was given a distinct entry and a separate physical presence (a separate card in a card catalogue). In automated catalogues, with the provision of keyword access (looking for a particular word or phrase contained anywhere in the catalogue record), the concept has apparently little value. However, it is still a useful tool to consider in constructing a catalogue and provides a structure around which cataloguing can take place successfully.

So what should a catalogue record look like? Normally, it should consist of a number of sections, the main ones of which are:

- a heading which is used as an access point for the item and the element which is used for filing the record;
- a description which identifies the item uniquely and tells you something of its nature (subject content, physical format, etc.);

- a shelfmark which identifies where in the collection the particular item is held (the classification mark as discussed in the previous chapter is often used for this purpose).

Each separate entry in the catalogue will be made up of a number of these features or sections which together will allow the user to identify whether or not the particular book they are looking for is in the collection. How you construct your catalogue will depend to a large extent on how your customers use it and how they go about the business of finding the information that they want. As in many other aspects of library work you need to adapt your systems to the way your customers are accustomed to working. However, there are a number of general rules which can be used to define what the functions of a catalogue should be.

Your catalogue should be built in a way that will enable library users to see if the library contains the particular item that they are looking for. It should therefore enable them to carry out the following operations:

- Find an item if they know the author, title or subject – obviously the greater the size of your collection the more difficult it will be to find an individual title by using only one of these (a large public library will have many hundreds of books by and about Shakespeare, for example) so that in practice it is more likely that one or more will be used in combination; author/title or author/subject will be necessary. It is also the case that in automated systems the use of keywords will allow successful retrieval if only part of the author, title or subject is known. But the general point of the catalogue as a finding list remains the case.

- Find out what the library has by a particular author, on a particular subject or in a particular format
- Assist in the choice of a particular book especially with regard to its edition.

These attributes were first described by Cutter in 1876[1] and still hold good today.

What elements to include in a cataloguing record

Following on from this, in order for your catalogue to fulfil those basic functions, the catalogue record itself will need to consist of a number of elements or fields which together will describe the item being catalogued in such a way that a user will be able to identify it immediately as the one they are looking for. What these elements should be will depend on the nature of the collection, the amount of time that you can afford to spend on the act of cataloguing and the way in which users approach the catalogue. The larger the collection is and the more diffuse your users the more complex individual catalogue records will need to be in order to sufficiently differentiate one title from another.

Librarians have been cataloguing material for a long time and, as a result, there is a long tradition behind the determination of what those elements or fields should be. No matter how simple you intend your catalogue to be it is worth considering these approaches in detail before deciding what you want to do. Perhaps the most familiar approach is the MARC (Machine Readable Cataloguing) record format which was designed in the late 1960s and which, since then, has been used as the standard format for representing this type of bibliographical information in a way which enables different types of library to store and then to communicate and reformat it in machine-readable form. The Library of Congress adopted the standard in 1968, followed by the British National Bibliography in 1971. The standard was designed so that it could represent different kinds of library material and be flexible enough to be used in all the situations where this information was needed.

Even if you do not wish to use MARC to its full extent, there are still a number of its elements that you may wish to consider for your catalogue, the most important of which are the following:

- *International Standard Book Number (ISBN).* This is a unique identifier given to books at the point of publication. It is a ten-digit number consisting of a publisher's prefix (usually the first six digits), a sequential number indicating the actual title and a check digit. It can be found on the back cover of the book and on the reverse of the title page. The majority of library management systems use this number as a unique reference point for creating catalogue records.

- *General Medium Designate (GMD).* This describes the format of the item being catalogued, whether, for example, the item is a book, a journal, a sound recording, an annual report, a map, and so on. Obviously, if your collection consists solely of maps then this element will be redundant. But in a mixed media collection, which most libraries will be, it is important for users to know the exact nature of the item in question. If a user wants the film version of Macbeth, for example, the printed text will be of no use to them.

- *Title*. The exact title of the item.

- *Author*. The person or persons responsible for the creation of the work in question, the writer of a book, the editor or compiler of a collection, the composer of a piece of music, the name of a performer.

- *Corporate author*. The name of the body responsible for the work in question in the absence of a personal author, for example the Department of Social Security.

- *Edition*. 1st, 2nd, revised and so on – essential information for detailing the exact currency of the item.

- *Place of publication*. Where the item was published or made available.

- *Publisher*. The name of the organisation responsible for publishing or issuing the item.

- *Year*. The year when the item originated.

- *Physical description*. The number of pages in a book, its size and whether or not it includes illustrations or maps etc.; alternatively the number of cassettes in a talking book, the length of a sound recording and so on.

- *Series title*. Information on similar material which has been grouped together in a particular way – Aslib Know How Guides, for example, or the Successful LIS Profession, or the Great Composers.

- *Series number*. The number of the item in that particular series.

- *Subject*. What the item is about.

- *Keywords*. Further subject identifiers which will aid retrieval.

- *Classification number*. The classification number assigned to the item by the cataloguer, usually denoting the overall subject content and the location of the item in the collection.

In addition to the fields above there are a number of other elements that you might wish to include that will give a fuller description of the item being catalogued. You need to decide for yourself how much detail you want to record but remember that you will need to assess the amount of time you spend on cataloguing against the additional benefit that your users will gain from the effort in terms of how more effective their searches will be as a result. This other information is usually held in the 'notes' field of a catalogue record. These notes come at the end of the record and some of the other factors that you may wish to include in these notes are:

- *Nature, scope or artistic form*. The precise nature of the item in question, e.g. a play in three acts, or a Latin reader.

- *Language*. The language the item is written in.

- *Source of title proper*. Where you found the title of the item if not from the title page or other normal source.

- *Physical description.* Those features of the item which have not been included already in the physical description area of your record but which are important for identification purposes. Examples of this sort of information might be, 'alternate pages blank' or 'limited edition of 120 numbered copies signed by the author'.

- *Summary.* A brief summary of the contents of the item.

There are other notes that could be included and the above list is not meant to be exhaustive but should be used to indicate the type of information which a user may find useful.

In considering your catalogue as a finding aid you will need to test it against the expectations of your users to see if the detail that you have included will be sufficient for them to find the items that they are looking for quickly and easily. In these terms the principles that Vickery[2] set down over 25 years ago still apply and can be very useful indeed in showing how effective your catalogue is or whether the automated system that you are using fulfils its basic functions. These principles can be stated in the following terms and are directly related to the basic features of a catalogue as described above. The catalogue should provide users with a way:

- to select items on the basis of the existence of character strings;

- to select items that are likely to be relevant to a particular topic;

- to select items that fall within a particular subject field;

- to rank selected records as to their relevance in a particular query;

- to order selected records in a meaningful way; and

- to aid searchers in their choice of subject terms to use.

If your catalogue enables your users to do all that, then you can assume that it is working in a satisfactory way. Performance can be measured in a number of different ways but perhaps the most relevant in this context are the following:

- recall – which is the ratio of items which fit the search criteria found to the number of items which fit the search criteria not found; and

- precision – which is the ratio of items which fit the search criteria found to the number of items which do not fit the search criteria found.

Anglo-American Cataloguing Rules

Reaching a decision on how you wish to describe items in your catalogue records and how you would wish those records to appear is, however, not the end of the matter. In order for the catalogue to work successfully it must be constructed in a consistent and coherent manner. And this is not necessarily as straightforward as it may appear. Sometimes it can be quite difficult to determine who is the actual author of a particular work or a particular author may have written under more than one name (the historical novelist, Jean Plaidy, wrote under several pen names for example). Authors may change names as Harold Macmillan did when he became the Earl of Stockton and yet it may be important for your users that the catalogue brings these various differences together in some way.

In other words you must construct the catalogue according to an agreed set of general rules or principles so that the internal integrity of the catalogue is maintained at all times. Information contained in the fields must be applied in the same way by everyone who is participating in the cataloguing process. Again, as you might expect, there is a long tradition of developing such rules and procedures within librarianship. Early attempts to codify rules for cataloguing were based on a 'cases' approach where specific rules were created to deal with specific situations. This caused some difficulties for cataloguers when they came across situations not covered by one of the rules and eventually another approach was developed that instead was based on a series of principles used to guide the cataloguer. The most relevant example of this 'conditions' approach was the Anglo-American Cataloguing Rules developed in 1967 (AACR1) and thoroughly revised in 1978 with further minor revisions in 1988 and 1998 (AACR2R2).

The difference between the two approaches is best exemplified by the way they deal with changes in an author's name. To take one example quoted in *Organizing Knowledge* by Jennifer Rowley and John Farrow[3] – the case of a woman changing her name on marriage is dealt with by the American Library Association 1949 rules in the following way:

Married women. Enter a married woman under the latest name unless, as specified below, she has consistently written under another name ...

A. When a woman uses her husband's forenames or initials in place of her own ... enter under her own name.

B. Omit the name of an earlier husband in the heading unless it continues to appear in the form of the name which the author customarily uses.

C. Enter a married woman who continues to write under her maiden name under the maiden name.

D. Enter a woman who remarries but continues to write under the name of a former husband under that name.

E. When a divorced woman resumes her maiden name, enter under the maiden name ...

And so on. Given that there are any number of reasons why individuals may change their name, each of which would have to be given a rule of their own in the 'cases' approach, it is easy to see how complicated such an approach can become. What the 'principles' approach does, however, is to simply recognise that in some cases a cataloguer will have to choose from among differing names and deals with it accordingly. AACR2 does this in the following way:

If a person has changed his or her name, choose the latest name or form of name unless there is reason to believe that an earlier name will persist as the name by which the person is better known.

AACR2R2 is available both in hard-copy and on CD-Rom. While the full application of these rules may not suit the particular library that you are trying to create, either due to its size of the amount of staff time that you have available for cataloguing, it is perhaps worth looking at how it is structured to see how its general principle can be applied as an aid for developing your own approach. For those wishing to avail themselves of a set of rules but without venturing into the complex world of AACR2R2 there is a British Standard on minimal cataloguing.[4]

The AACR2R2 rules are designed to follow the sequence of a cataloguers' work and to describe the item being catalogued in detail, moving from the general to the specific. This sequence can be characterised as follows:

- *Description*. This means creating a description of the item based on the chief source of information about it (generally the title page if it is a book). This description should contain enough information to explain the access points (called headings in AACR2R2) under which it is filed.

- *Choice of access points*. This follows the description and is best described as the manner by which items are searched for by users. An access point can therefore be either an author or a corporate author, and any given work is likely to have more than just one access point.

- *Headings*. The particular name or variant of a name or filing element that the cataloguer chooses to use when more than one is available.

- *Reference*. The way the cataloguer guides users to the chosen heading from all other potential headings using *see* references to direct users from an unused heading to a used one and *see also* references to direct users to other relevant information held under a different heading.

It is beyond the scope of this publication to consider in greater detail the complexity of AACR2R2. If you wish to explore this area further then an excellent starting point can be found in *Essential Cataloguing* by J.H. Bowman.[5]

Computerised cataloguing systems

The majority of library cataloguing is nowadays carried out through library management systems with access to users being provided through Online Public Access Catalogues (OPACs). Originally, access to the OPAC was through a dedicated terminal in the library but with the greater flexibility afforded by computer networking, access can now be done on an individual basis either at the desktop or remotely through a modem. In addition, with improvements made to information retrieval and the interface between computers and users, many libraries are offering access to library collections other than their own: either by taking advantage of the many library collections available over the Internet or by developing arrangements with other libraries to share collections.

Library management systems themselves are usually constructed on a modular basis as this flexibility allows the library to prioritise needs and is especially important if you are working on a limited budget. A modular approach also allows the library to determine which elements are to be introduced when, and thus facilitates the training of both staff and users in an ordered and timely fashion. This approach is not without problems, however, especially if you purchase the various modules over an extended period of time. As these systems are constantly evolving, the new modules you buy may not work properly with the old modules you already have without further work and possible additional costs as well.

While different library management systems bring their own approach to automating library work (and you will have to decide which approach is best suited to your library) they all consist of the same basic elements or modules. These are:

- cataloguing – to enable you to create records of what the library holds and make it available to users;

- circulation – to enable you to record who has borrowed a particular item and how long they are allowed to hold it for;

- enquiry – to enable users to interrogate the library catalogue;

- acquisitions – to enable library staff to create records of items which are on order and to provide the means of sending orders to suppliers and update the library's budget records;

- serials – to manage the cataloguing of serial titles and to provide routing slips if the library circulates its serials to a number of different users;

- management – to allow a systems administrator to decide how the library management system is to work and what parts of it can be accessed by particular members of staff or users.

Cataloguing through these systems is achieved either by the system supplying a template with headings for staff to complete (an on-screen form containing headings such as author, title, etc., some of which must be completed before progress can be made) or by a mechanism which allows the system administrator to determine in advance how the library is going to catalogue its holdings and supplying a template of the library's choosing. Again you will have to decide which approach is best suited to your particular library based on the number of staff available for cataloguing and their proficiency as cataloguers.

Notes

1. C.A. Cutter (1904) *Rules for a Dictionary Catalogue*, 4th edn. Government Printing Office.
2. B.C. Vickery (1971) 'Structure and function in retrieval languages', *Journal of Documentation*, 27(2), 69–82.
3. Jennifer Rowley and John Farrow (2002) *Organizing Knowledge: An Introduction to Managing Access to Information*, 3rd edn. Ashgate.
4. British Standards Institution: BS 5605: 1990 Recommendations for citing and referencing published materials.
5. J.H. Bowman (2003) *Essential Cataloguing*. Facet Publishing.

Further reading

Akers, Susan G. (1969) *Simple Library Cataloguing*. Scarecrow Press.

Burke, Mary A. (1999) *Organization of Multimedia Resources: Principles and Practice of Information Retrieval*. Ashgate.

Byrne, Deborah J. (1998) *MARC Manual: Understanding and Using MARC Records*. Libraries Unlimited.

Harbour, Robin T. (1994) *Managing Library Automation*. Aslib.

Hill, R.W. (1999) *Setting the Record Straight: A Guide to the MARC Format*. British Library.

Mortimer, Mary (2001) *Learn Descriptive Cataloguing*, Workbooks for Learning Cataloguing and Classification Schemes. Scarecrow Press.

Read, Jane (2003) *Cataloguing Without Tears: Managing Knowledge in the Information Society*. Chandos Publishing.

6

Providing additional material for your users – the art of stock selection

In this chapter we will take a closer look at stock provision and the art of stock selection. By this stage in the project you will have already created the nucleus of your collection and now that your library material has been arranged on the shelves in classified order and catalogued, you need to start thinking more about how you can extend the range of material that you have made available to users either by further acquisition or by introducing a system to obtain information from other libraries or commercial suppliers.

We have already discussed this to some degree in an earlier chapter. In Chapter 3 we examined the various ways in which information is used and concluded that, in general terms, users need access to:

- information which is current;
- information which is specific to the functions that they carry out;
- general information relating to news and current affairs;
- information which will help them improve the work they do;
- information for general reading.

We noted too that this information will be found in a number of different formats among which the most common would be:

■ books

■ journals

■ newspapers

■ reports

■ electronic databases.

This was discussed in the context of trying to identify users' information needs and while it obviously holds true, identifying what your users need is only part of the way in which a library should respond to the question of stock provision. What is also of crucial importance is to determine how to meet that need out of the array of material that is available, often in more than one format. The world of information supply is a complex one and getting more complex all the time. Indeed, it is this very complexity which gives libraries and librarians such an important role in a whole range of modern organisations and institutions.

One of the major roles you should try to play in this situation is to develop sufficient knowledge and expertise about the information world that enables you to act as a bridge (or gateway as it is sometimes called) between what users need and the information sources that are available to meet those needs. By ensuring that the most appropriate material is acquired in the most appropriate format you will be providing a service for users that will save them time and money and contribute directly to the efficiency of your parent organisation.

However, stock does not select itself. It needs to be evaluated before selection and then promoted after selection. This is what we will consider in this chapter by looking at how information is produced and by developing criteria for evaluating it.

Library budgets

No library, no matter how well funded, can afford to buy everything that is produced that might be considered relevant to meeting the needs of users. There is simply too much information available for that. The competing demands of users and the depth and variety of those demands must be managed within a budget that will probably be too small for you to be able to acquire everything that you would like and within a library space that will not be as big as you first imagined. Decisions will have to be made about the size of any budget for stock that you are given and then priorities established for spending it in the most appropriate way.

Deciding the size of your required budget in the initial phase of starting a new library service will be difficult as you will have no real idea about what the demands on your service will be once the service is established, and how much stock you will need to meet those demands. What you should have established, however, from the information audit is how much your organisation is already spending on providing information for staff. This figure can be used as a baseline for the first couple of years in the life of the new service and then money either surrendered or new bids made depending on how much you were given in the first place, how the service has developed and how well you have been able to establish the benefits of the service in the minds of those who have to pay for it.

However you have to present it, the budget process will then take the following form:

- making an annual bid to cover the cost incurred in purchasing library material based on an analysis of information need and the previous year's budget;
- determining how to spend the budget across various spending headings;
- monitoring how the budget was spent and the value to the organisation of the library's spending activity.

How this monitoring is done will be discussed in Chapter 8 on performance measurement.

Whatever your budget you will still need to decide how to spend it and how to balance the different needs of your various users. In particular you will need to consider how much of your budget should be spent on:

- books as opposed to serials;
- print material as opposed to electronic information;
- ownership as opposed to access.

The answers to these questions will depend on the sort of library you wish to establish and the extent and variety of the information needs of your users. This will, of course, vary from library to library but there are a number of common elements that should be considered in trying to reach a meaningful conclusion:

- the size of library space available (how much material you can physically store);
- the number of library staff (for processing material and getting it to users);
- the distribution of your users (in one building convenient to the library, in a number of buildings close together, in a widely spread out organisation);
- on how connected the organisation is (for networking electronic information).

This information will allow you to make some tentative decisions about how to allocate the budget which you have been given. As the service develops your budget allocation can be modified in the light of what you have learned in the process. You need to think carefully about this because there is no point in spending the bulk of your budget on providing a large roomful of expensive texts, for example, when most of your users never visit the library and want access to the information they need from their desktop. You also need to be prepared to be flexible. Even if you think you have got the information 'fit' correct it does not mean that it will be correct for all time and in all circumstances. User needs change, as does the way in which information is produced. And you need to be able to change in response to this so that you can act quickly and flexibly as a consequence.

Acquisition policy/collection development policy

As this is a new service you may wish to develop a formal acquisition or collection development policy as an aid to decision-making. While the advantages of such formal approaches are not clear-cut, particularly if the documentation used is vague, a well thought-out approach will at least give you the chance to inform users of what the library is trying to do in this area and the sorts of information that the library will and will not make available through purchase. A good collections development policy should define:

- the core subject area of the library's collection;
- what additional information will be made available;
- the total resources available for the library to spend on information provision and the way it is being allocated;
- how long the information will be held for;
- how users can access the information;
- how users can inform the acquisitions process and help influence the collections policy.

It should also inform users of any particular initiatives the library is going to introduce on a yearly basis to strengthen the collection in certain areas, for example, or to invest more than usual in a particular format (a move from provision of printed serials to more investment in electronic serials, for example).

Holdings versus access

One of the things that you will need to decide as part of your acquisitions policy is how far your library will seek to acquire and own the information that your users need rather than obtain it from another library or a third-party supplier on loan. It goes without saying that no library can ever expect to own everything that users will require and that inter-library lending is an essential component of all library services and systems. This has always been the case. However, there are a number of factors at the moment that make this of immediate concern for libraries, particularly for those engaged in starting a new library service. This is another aspect of the complexity of the information world. The factors which should be considered here include:

- the sheer scale of the amount of information that continues to be published;
- the cost of acquiring the information and the rise in price which over the past ten years has consistently been higher than the general rate of inflation;
- the pressures on library funding;
- the pressures to make economies on library space;
- the wider availability of information held electronically and the increased demands that awareness of these sources make on library services.

These factors are pushing libraries more towards what has been termed the access model and the creation of virtual libraries. In this model the library maintains a core collection (essentially 'must have' material which is either consulted frequently or which the organisation simply cannot do without) and then provides access to a variety of other information databases where information is made available on demand.

On the face of it such arrangements appear to be cost-effective in that library resources are not tied up in acquiring and storing material which is rarely or never used, but there are costs associated with such a model in terms of setting up systems and paying for document supply, some of which may be considerable. In fact the access model is far from perfect and it does have its limitations. It suffers from some quite serious drawbacks and these need to be considered in the context of the sort of service that users might expect. Things which you may wish to consider here are:

- the problems associated with the delay in supplying materials that the library does not hold;
- the fact that the model precludes user browsing;
- the possibility that individual items not in stock may be requested by users on more than one occasion.

As a result it is very difficult to determine in every case whether it is more appropriate for a library to buy rather than to borrow and judgements will need to be made in terms of balancing different factors, including:

- the costs involved in buying;
- the costs involved in borrowing;
- the level of likely use of the individual item;
- the consequence for the organisation of any delay in supply;
- the value of the material over time.

Thinking of library provision in this way will help you to decide what the core 'must have' material is for you and what material can be safely obtained from elsewhere.

Stock selection

The next stage, following on from the development of your acquisitions policy and decisions relating to your core collection, is to consider how best to decide what individual items you should be purchasing from all the material that is available. We will consider each of the various formats in turn beginning with printed monographs (books).

Printed monographs

In trying to decide whether a particular title fits in with your overall acquisitions policy you need to find out as much as possible about it. This information will include details about the price, the date of publication and the physical characteristics of the book, and something about its content and overall subject matter. This sort of detail can be found in a number of sources by looking at:

- the information supplied by publishers;
- reviews;
- advertisements;
- features in trade publications;
- listings in various bibliographies.

By using some or all of these sources you will be able to make an informed judgement about the usefulness for your library of particular items in the majority of cases. In this way some items will select themselves due to their importance for the particular organisation, while others will simply be too expensive to consider under any circumstances.

This would seem to suggest that the process of stock selection at this level is a relatively straightforward exercise. Unfortunately, this is not the case as not all of the information that you need will be available when you need it. One of the most annoying habits of publishers is to advertise material for publication weeks (sometimes months) in advance, and while some reviews will appear contemporaneously with publication others will follow a good time later. This leaves the question open as to when is the best time to purchase a new publication?

Obviously, the more information that you have about a particular publication the better. This is particularly true if you are operating with only a limited budget and you are worried about spending it on publications that may or may not fit your user profile. This would appear to indicate that selection several weeks after publication when a number of reviews have already appeared will be the most successful because by then you will be more or less certain whether the publication is going to be useful to purchase. However, this will not always be the case. There are a number of other pressures which favour early selection and which you will need to take into consideration as well. These include:

- user expectation – if a publication is well publicised in advance then users will expect it to appear on the library shelves immediately on publication. Failure to do this may reflect badly on how users perceive the efficiency and value of the library;
- the fact that some publications have a notoriously short print-run so that any delay in ordering may result in failure to acquire sufficient copies;
- the possibility that some publications may get overlooked completely while library staff wait for the most appropriate reviews to appear.

As with much library work what you need to do is to try to achieve an appropriate balance between spending quickly so that the library stock always appears fresh and dynamic and having sufficient information about a publication so that mistakes can be eliminated or at least kept to a minimum.

You can do this by building up your subject knowledge of the areas you are concentrating on (knowing the authors who are the acknowledged specialists in the field and the publications where the best reviews appear) and by concentrating your selection on one single source (possibly a trade listing, a specialist supplier, a particular periodical or a national bibliography) and augmenting this information with some of the other sources listed above. If you have a number of staff working for you then they can be given particular responsibility for certain subject areas or responsibility for looking at reviews in particular periodicals in order to develop the subject knowledge which is at the heart of good selection policy. If subject areas are sufficiently well defined this approach will also help cut down on the potential duplication of orders and the subsequent waste of money that this involves.

You need to remember too that it is particularly difficult to assess the value of any publication that you purchase. While it is perhaps gratifying for a library to see something that it has purchased being borrowed a number of times this does not necessarily mean that it represents value for money for the parent organisation. Value can only be determined by the effect that a publication has on the person who reads it and the changes that might be introduced to the way the organisation does things as a result. In this sort of situation a publication read by only one person inspiring dramatic change will have more value than a publication read by a number of people which changes nothing.

Printed serials

The next element that you need to consider after printed monographs are serials (journals and other periodicals) and how expenditure on them relates to general expenditure on books. The ISO standard 329 defines a serial as a publication 'issued in successive parts usually having numerical or chronological designations, and intended to be continued indefinitely'. The main feature of a serial in a library context is that its frequency of appearance (either on a daily, weekly, monthly, quarterly or annual basis, to take only the most common examples) allows it to present information that will be much more current than the information that is usually found in books. As a consequence of this serial, publications are used primarily:

- as a vehicle for presenting research findings as soon as they are available;
- as a means of informing practitioners in a wide range of activities of the latest news in their particular field.

These two functions are sometimes difficult to differentiate as the concept of news and research overlap to some degree but a good example of how they are used can be found by considering the *British Medical Journal* and the *Lancet*. The brief reports of recent research which they contain are essential reading for medical practitioners and other researchers who wish to be kept up to date with recent developments in their fields. As you would expect, the most relevant publishers of such material are learned societies and professional associations, although some commercial publishers are also active in the field.

The nature of the organisation that you work for and the importance of staff being kept up to date will determine the extent to which your organisation will be dependent on the information found in serial publications in comparison with that found in monographs. You will need to decide, based on this knowledge, the proportion of your budget that will be spent on each. You will have gained some insight into how your organisation works during the information audit phase of the project but it is likely that if you work in a specialist or government sector then the greater proportion will be spent on the acquisition of serial publications – because it is the latest information which will have the most value for staff.

It is likely too that there will be a requirement for you to provide access to the contents of serials to library users by circulating the actual journals to them. If you are required to do this then it will tend to increase the number of copies of any serial being circulated as you will not wish circulation lists to have too many names on them or the time taken to circulate them will be too long. This is not a particularly satisfactory way of ensuring that your serials are well used – once a particular journal leaves the library the library loses control over it and does not know if any actual circulation is taking place or if the journal will ever return. This also makes it difficult to retain comprehensive holdings of important journals.

There are alternative ways of keeping users up to date that you might wish to consider instead: such as circulating contents pages only or abstracting the contents of important articles yourself and then providing photocopies of articles on request but in both instances you should also consider the limitations placed on you by copyright law. This is something considered further in Appendix B.

Electronic information

One of the major changes that libraries have been faced with in recent years is the way in which information is being published and the variety of different electronic formats that now exist. Such is the pace of this change that it is difficult for even the most well informed librarian to be sure how best to assess the value of the different formats or to decide which of the formats is likely to have the most assured future. Some attempt will need to be made, however, given the growing importance that users place on getting direct access to the information they require. In this situation you will need to decide:

- how spending should be balanced between expenditure on print material and expenditure on electronic material;
- how spending should be balanced on expenditure on the various electronic products available (CD-Rom or online databases).

You will need to base these decisions not only on the availability of the information itself but also on a number of factors relating to the context in which your library is operating such as:

- the number and location of staff using the library;
- the assistance library staff give to users in finding information;
- the availability and robustness of computer networks;
- the familiarity of users with computers and their knowledge of the various electronic systems available;
- the availability of training;
- overall library budget and size and location of the library.

By looking at these factors you will be able to determine how easily the provision of information in electronic format fits in with the working practices of your organisation. In some organisations the role of the library will be restricted to simply providing access to the information sources which will then be exploited by the users themselves, while in others library staff will still be expected to use the information sources to provide answers to specific user questions. You need to decide to what extent your library fits into either model and what implications this will have for library spending.

In some respects the same criteria that were used to evaluate printed material can be used to evaluate electronic information sources, particularly price. The main problem for librarians trying to gauge value for money is that the way in which information provision is developing means that finding the right information for users is becoming increasingly complex. The same information, or what appears to be the same information, can often be found in a variety of formats:

- in print;
- on CD-Rom;
- on the Internet;
- via online hosts.

Each of these will have a different emphasis on detail, currency and layout. Some will be easier to use than others, some more readily available and each will have a different pricing structure with not all of the costs being apparent at the point of purchase. As well as trying to develop an overall policy on the extent to which information provision will be based on access to electronic sources, you will also have to make individual decisions on a continuous basis on the extent to which you will rely on these sources to meet specific requests for information. The factors which you should consider here in trying to develop a sensible way out of this complexity will include the following:

- *Frequency of use* – is there likely to be a continuing need for users to gain access to a particular database or information product and how will use effect the cost of the product?

- *Number of users* – will there be a number of people who will need to gain access to the information at any given time and will the organisation suffer if this cannot be achieved?

- *Information retrieval* – will users know exactly what they want from the information source or will they need facilities (or help) with sophisticated searching.

- *Currency* – will users need access to current information only or will they need continued access to archived sources?

- *Usage* – will users interpret the information online or will there be a requirement to print out copies of what they find to consult later?

The answers to these questions will help you decide what is the most appropriate way of supplying information to users and help them make the best use out of it. Whatever else you decide, the needs and capabilities of users are the most important factors that need to be taken into consideration.

Electronic serials

One of the major growth areas in electronic publishing over recent years has been the expansion of the number of serial titles that are available in electronic format – either as a CD-Rom or increasingly from an online database through the Internet. Journals published in this way offer many advantages over traditional serial publications, among the more obvious of which are the following:

- *Ease of access.* In theory, depending on the licensing arrangements that govern your acquisition, an electronic serial will give instant and continuous access to your users at all times. Users will not be inconvenienced by a search for a particular title that someone else may have, or which may be lost or missing, or has been sent to the bindery. If sufficient network arrangements are in place they will be available from the desktop as well as the library and enhanced search facilities will make it easier for users to find the exact information that they require. That being said it is still true that users are resistant to reading long articles from a screen and that printing costs will increase as more articles are printed off for use. This may result in the library incurring extra costs and may present some difficulties with copyright legislation.

- *Shelving.* With electronic serials available in a continuous way there may no longer be any requirement for the library to store serials over a long period, thus reducing costs for storage and for binding if that was once required. However, there is still little practical experience of making the contents of electronic serials available over long periods of time and this may present you will difficulties in the future. There is also the additional problem that access to the information is only guaranteed as long as you continue to pay the subscription. The library does not own the information in the way it did when it purchased printed serials but leases access to it. This may cause difficulties if, for some reason, the library had to cancel the subscription to a particular serial.

- *Speed of publication.* The advent of electronic serials with their ability to circumvent traditional methods of publishing and distribution has certainly speeded up the whole publishing process with material reaching users much more quickly. This is particularly important in those fields such as science and medicine when there is an obvious benefit in disseminating research findings as quickly as impossible. There remains the danger, however, of the refereeing process not being able to cope with the demand for immediate publication and the possibility of information being released before it is quite ready.

How to provide access to electronic serials

Despite these problems it is likely that you will need to provide access to electronic serials as part of the developing library service. To add to the complexity of the situation there are a number of different approaches that can be adopted in providing access to electronic serials for your users, each of which have a number of advantages and disadvantages. The most common approaches take the following forms:

■ *Subscriptions to single titles.* This usually arises when a serial for which you will have an existing subscription also becomes available in electronic format either as part of the subscription or for a very small additional cost. Subscriptions on this basis will usually:

  – allow access from a single library terminal and the possibility of networking;

  – provide users with a table of contents;

  – provide access to the full text of articles;

  – allow users to fully search the database.

■ *A site licence from a publisher.* Licences taken on this basis will usually have the following features:

  – they will allow users to access either the complete range of titles from that particular publisher or from predetermined subject clusters;

  – they will be free at the point of use for searching, viewing and downloading;

  – they will provide unlimited copying within an organisation.

■ *A subscription service provided by an intermediary (usually a subscription agency).* The intermediary in this situation will organise the licensing aspects required for you, acting in the traditional sense of a subscription agent. The intermediary will provide a single interface and password for all the titles available from the publishers hosted by the intermediary whether or not your library has taken an actual subscription to any of the individual titles involved. This means that in addition to the features described above, for those titles that the library does have a subscription for you will be able:

- to search the contents and abstracts of the titles for which you have no subscription;
- to purchase copies of articles on an individual basis;
- to allow users to take advantage of the various alerting services that the intermediary may provide.

The main difference with this last approach is that the searchable database will contain many thousands of titles. On the one hand this will be of benefit to your users by giving them access to material previously denied to them, but on the other hand it will also increase the complexity of the tasks involved in managing this access, particularly in term of the potential impact that widening out access will have on library budgets. As users become aware of new information, demand for it is likely to increase and if it clearly falls within your acquisitions framework then it may be difficult for you to try and put limits on it, whether you allow users to purchase it straight from the database, or whether you try to obtain it instead from another library. As you have no real idea about the quantities of material that will be obtained as a result it makes planning library expenditure much more difficult.

The Internet

The subject of the Internet hardly needs an introduction such is its seeming dominance of the information world. However, it is worth considering for a moment in this chapter as the provision of so much information through the Internet, much of it free, a lot of it very useful but also a great deal of it unreliable, does have an impact on the way libraries perform their functions, and particularly how they provide information to their users.

The Internet in its simplest terms is a collection of interlinked computer networks which, when accessed from an individual computer, gives that user the ability to find information located on any computer linked to one of the networks. For many years it was essentially an academic network but it has been gradually adapted for business use and is now an essential part of the daily lives of many people. When speaking of the Internet some people use the term World Wide Web instead. In strict terms the two are not synonymous, with the World Wide Web being only those servers which link to the Internet using the hypertext transfer protocol (HTTP). However, this is not the place to discuss the technical aspects of the Internet, how it works and what its essential components are. It is sufficient for our purposes to note that a growing number of people rely on it as a significant source for accessing the information that they need and that this will have a major impact on libraries and how they deliver their services.

In this regard our main source of interest is the information which individuals and institutions are making available through the World Wide Web and in particular those reference sources which traditionally many people would have accessed only through their library. With this information now being readily available from an individual's own computer, the role that the library traditionally played in aspects of information provision is now being questioned and doubts cast about whether it has a long-term future. If users can access the information for themselves what do they need libraries for?

As you are in the middle of just starting a new library service this is probably something that you do not want to hear! In order to consider this question further we need to look more closely at the types of information that we are talking about. A list of such information would consist of some of the following, a mix of information that is available free and information for which a charge is made:

- information from organisations, companies and other corporate bodies about the work they do and the services they provide;

- information from government departments and other political institutions about the work they do and the services they provide including access to parliamentary debates, Acts of Parliament, green and white papers;

- advice on legal, health and other matters and concerns relating to the needs of citizens operating in a modern society;

- information from learned societies including access to research work that they have commissioned;

- the texts of newspapers and periodicals from both Britain and abroad and a growing number of electronic journals (some of which do not have print equivalents);

- a number of the standard reference books (the *Oxford English Dictionary*, for example), yearbooks and directories;

- a range of information about news and currents affairs (*BBC Online*, for example) which support other media outputs;

- weather reports;

- transport information;

- information supporting hobbies, pastimes and sporting activities;

- information about local groups and the activities they undertake.

The list is actually endless. Whatever activity you can think of you will be able to find an Internet site somewhere that is devoted to it. And that is the crux of the problem. Because anyone can put information onto the Internet, because there is no overarching body responsible for controlling and authenticating it, and because there is so much of it, it makes it very difficult indeed for someone to find information that is actually useful, or in the case of some information (help and advice on matters relating to health, for example) that is not implicitly misleading or downright dangerous.

There is also a problem with the stability of information: information that you managed to find once but could not find again when you went back to it because of the number of sites:

- which change address without alerting you to the fact or directing your browser to the new address;

- which disappear completely;

- which no longer hold the information that you were looking for.

This is compounded by the difficulty of access during certain times of the day and sites which are temporarily (but always when you need them) unavailable because they are undergoing maintenance or experiencing technical difficulties.

These problems and the sheer scale of the information provision concerned present librarians with opportunities as well as threats in that they can exploit their stock selection skills in this new area. If the main skill of a librarian is in identifying the information needs of library users and then arranging that information in a way which is accessible to them, then this is exactly the skill that is needed in helping users to navigate their way through the World Wide Web. By using these skills to evaluate the contents of Internet sites you will be able to supplement the information resources and services that you are providing directly to users with mediated access to web-based information and to sites which your users will have confidence in using.

Through understanding the information needs of your users you will be able to determine what sites are potentially useful. These sites should be evaluated by looking at:

- the purpose of the site, its overall coverage and whether its intended audience is a business, academic, professional or popular one;
- the authority of the site, whether it originates from an agency that can be held to account for the accuracy of the information it contains, a government department, an academic institution, a professional body, a learned society, or a named author who is a recognised expert in the field;

- its inclusion in subject gateways (lists of sites that have been approved by information or subject specialists using known selection criteria, such as SOSIG – the Social Science Information Gateway) or other mechanisms for reviewing and appraising sites;
- the links it might contain to other approved sites.

Other things that might act as a pointer to the reliability of information contained on websites would also include:

- the availability of the site over time;
- the frequency of updates and the inclusion of information about when these updates last occurred or when particular items were first published;
- the number of links to and from other sites previously approved by you;
- the number of links to other sites which no longer work;
- the ease with which users can navigate their way around the site to find the information they require;
- the reliability of search engines in helping users find the information they require.

Once you have evaluated a site and included it in your list of library approved sites you need to check it periodically to make sure that it is still functioning properly and is still valuable as this will not always be the case. By undertaking this work on behalf of users you will be reinforcing the traditional library role of providing access to information (or information gatekeeper as it is sometimes called), reinforcing the value of the service that you operate and maintaining user loyalty.

A useful tool to help you understand the complexity of the issues involved in evaluating Internet sites is provided by the SOSIG gateway noted above. It provides an interactive tutorial on evaluating the quality of Internet resources at: *http://www.sosig.ac.uk/internet_detective.html*.

Further reading

Chambers, J. (1999) 'End-user document supply or who needs an inter-library loans service?', *Interlending and Document Supply*, 27(2), 71–9.

Kidd, Tony and Rees-Jones, Lyndsay (2000) *The Serials Management Handbook: A Practical Guide to Print and Electronic Serials Management*. Library Association Publishing.

Martin, Murray S. (1995) *Collection Development and Finance: Materials Budgeting*. American Library Association.

Pantry, Sheila and Griffiths, Peter (2002) *Creating a Successful E.information Service*. Facet Publishing.

Rowley, J. (1998) *The Electronic Library*. Library Association Publishing.

Shreeves, Edward (1991) *Guide to Budget Allocation for Information Resources, A Collection Management and Development Guide*. American Library Association.

Spiller, David (2000) *Providing Materials for Library Users*. Library Association Publishing.

7

Planning further service development

In this chapter we will consider how to plan the future development of the library and look at a range of services that your library could offer in addition to maintaining the collection of books and other information sources that you have acquired. What you will be able to do is, of course, dependent to a large extent on the number of staff working with you in the library and the resources that you have been given but whatever those numbers and resources an element of planning will still be essential if you are to make the best use of your situation.

What is planning?

There is no fixed definition of what planning is in a library context although in general terms it can be described as the process which enables the library to consider how its activities can be adapted to meet the needs of its parent organisation. It means developing an understanding of the purpose of the library within that context, setting objectives for the library which meet the needs of the organisation as a whole, formulating a plan which stipulates how those objectives will be met and then implementing the plan in all its detail. This is, however, a continuous process with both formulation and implementation changing over time in response to changes either within the library itself or within the parent organisation. Indeed, the planning process can be considered as the mechanism by which the library adapts itself to the changing environment in which it operates.

This is something that every library will have to do whether or not it decides to do it through a formal library plan. The main benefits of producing such a plan for someone engaged in the process of starting a new library service are that:

- it will help clarify what it is that the library should be doing and what objectives it should set itself;
- it will help decide the range of services the library should be developing and how important they are in meeting the overall objectives;
- it will help provide an overall policy framework against which decisions can be judged;
- it will help identify the resources that will be needed for the library to meet its objectives;
- it will help identify any obstacles which may prevent the library from meeting its objectives.

By clarifying in this way what the main purpose and objectives of the new library are and by stating how library operations will help the parent organisation meet its own strategic objectives you will be in a better position to argue for the funds that you will need to deliver the services identified in the plan. If, at the same time, you can involve library users in defining what the objectives of the library should be and in defining the services that will be required to meet those objectives, then you are more likely to find supporters within the organisation who will also help argue for the necessary funding. The participation of library users within the planning process will also help you to respond more quickly to changing needs and encourage a flexible approach to information provision.

There are many approaches that can help you with the business of strategic planning (for more information see the list of books in the further reading section at the end of this chapter) and no one is really any better than any other. What is involved is finding answers to a range of questions about the situation of the library and the parent organisation and then fitting the results within an overall strategic framework. It may help to consider this using the following headings:

- *Analysis* – a detailed examination of how the library fits in with the work of the parent organisation.

- *Assumptions* – the assumptions you make about the role of the library in the work of the parent organisation (that staff within the organisation need access to accurate, up-to-date information to carry out their basic functions, for example, or that funding will continue at such and such a level).

- *Key questions that you need to ask* – why should the library exist? what should it be doing? who should be doing it? how should they do it?

- *Mandates* – where does the authority of the library come from?

- *Strategic themes* – what strategic themes emerge from consideration of the key questions?

- *Barriers* – what are the things (shortage of staff, shortage of resources) that would prevent the library from fulfilling its strategic objectives?

- *Challenges* – what are the main challenges that will be faced by the library in trying to meet those objectives?

- *Outcomes* – how will the library know that the objectives have been met?

As you go through the various headings a picture will start to emerge of how the library is positioned within your parent organisation and of the factors which must be taken into consideration when planning further activities. If you have undertaken the exercise in a considered fashion you should be able to start the process of translating the information obtained into the rudiments of a plan by stating in a clear and concise way:

- the overall purpose of the library and what its unique contribution to the organisation is;

- who the users of the library are and how the library relates to them;

- what the resources of the library are in terms of staff and other resources;

- what the objectives of the library should be;

- the level of services that the library needs to develop in order to meet those objectives;

- how the library (and library users) will judge whether or not the objectives have been met.

Taken together this will provide a strategic framework for your library, providing a series of goals and objectives and the context in which individual tasks will operate. It should be noted here, however, that these individual tasks will not flow directly from the framework as there will always be more than one way to accomplish a particular goal. You will still need to choose how to proceed although you will now be in a better position to do so.

In some planning schemas the operation of specific tasks is often considered to be part of the action plan rather than part of the strategic planning framework. This does not seem advisable to me as lists of tasks make little sense when isolated in this way. As part of the strategic planning framework each specific task should be organised to provide the following detail:

- how each task will be undertaken;
- what the desired outcome will be;
- who will be responsible for undertaking it;
- what the other resource implications are;
- when the task will begin;
- when will it be completed.

Considering both aspects of the planning process in this way (the strategic with the operational) also creates the necessary link between the long-term goals of the service and the realities of day-to-day activities. If this link is not made then there is the danger of either long-term goals disappearing in the face of pressure to get on with delivering frontline services or of more and more work being forced on already pressurised staff for no apparent reason. When considered together, individual tasks are given new meaning and new emphasis because the ways in which they relate to the overall purpose of the library have been clearly stated.

This leaves the question of monitoring which is considered in Chapter 8 on performance measurement.

Service development

In order to ensure that the new service becomes something more than just a collection of material that has been put in the library because no one wants it any longer, you will need to consider, as part of the planning process, how to increase the range and scope of the services that you offer to users. There are a number of basic library services which are more or less common to all libraries and others that can be amended or adapted to meet your particular circumstances. However, many of these services can be costly and so before any particular service is introduced you need to have weighed up these factors properly so that you have the resources, including staffing resources, available to manage them over time. There is nothing worse than introducing new services which the library then has to abandon because it does not have sufficient time or money to continue providing them.

It is much better developing an initially small range of basic services and then building on that as time and resources allow. Some services you will not be able to develop without additional staffing; but seeing how they fit in with existing services and the benefits they will bring to the service as a whole will allow you to build up a business case at a later stage when you think it appropriate to do so.

Circulation

This is probably the most basic feature of all library services but one which you will still need to plan carefully. The main premise for starting the new library service in the first place was that the staff in your organisation needed access to information and the only way they could do this under prevailing conditions was to acquire and then hold that information themselves. This led to the inefficiencies detailed in Chapter 1 which the creation of a library service was designed to overcome. In part, what this means at the most basic level was that the library would assume responsibility for acquiring the information that staff required, arranging it so that it could be retrieved on a systematic basis (classification and cataloguing) and then making it available to staff when they needed it.

Libraries make the information available to staff either by holding it in a central location for staff to consult at that central location (reference services) or by allowing staff to remove the information either on a short-term or longer-term basis (circulation services) while recording the details of the information on loan to them. If you decide to provide such a service you will need to develop a system that accurately records the details of the loans against the person who is borrowing them. This is usually done through the sort of library management system (LMS) described in Chapter 5 on cataloguing, although if such a system is not available to you there are a number of paper-based alternatives (a simple journal, for example, or the issuing of library tickets to each borrower) that you could use.

Whatever the method of recording there are a number of other matters that you need to decide before any circulation system will function properly. These will include decisions on:

- whether all your material should be made available for loan or whether some important information which a number of staff will need to consult on a continuous basis (law texts, for example) should be considered as part of the reference collection only available through consultation in the library;

- how much material you will allow to be on loan to any one individual at any one time – you can decide on an arbitrary figure or simply let anyone borrow as much as they like, or you can create different rules for different categories of staff so that a trainee, for example, is not allowed to borrow as much as the chief executive. There is no correct answer to either of these questions as it will depend entirely on your individual circumstances. You should, however, try to exercise some element of control as the more material on loan that is not being used productively the less efficient the overall library service becomes;

- whether all your material should be on loan for the same period – rather than make some information reference only you could establish overnight or short-term loan categories for sought after material and even allow some which is considered as being on permanent loan;

- whether to record when material should be returned, send out reminders for material not returned and take steps to recover material still out on loan despite these reminders – if you do decide to issue reminders then the wording used in any reminder letter will be crucial. Remember that in the past circumstances of your organisation staff will not have been used to the concept of 'borrowing' and 'sharing' this type of information and that an ill-conceived letter may undo months of hard preparation and planning.

Together the answers to these questions will form your library's circulation policy. You should take steps to make sure that this policy is approved by senior management within your organisation and that staff are informed about how the policy will work in practice.

Enquiry services

This is the other main element of the library service involving library staff in utilising library stock to answer information enquiries from users. While work in this area can be difficult it will provide you with some of the most interesting challenges you are likely to get in operating a new library service. It should also be pointed out that the success and reputation of the library as a whole will invariably be judged on the quality of its enquiry service and care must be taken to carry out duties here in a thoroughly professional manner.

The enquiry service needs to be accessible to users at all times and should be set up to allow them to communicate with the library in the way that suits them, whether in person, by phone, by fax or by e-mail. The various ways in which the service can be contacted need to be publicised throughout the organisation and detailed in any promotional material that you produce.

This is particularly the case with a new service. Library users will not be accustomed to the provision of such a service nor aware of what it could do for them. All the hard work of organising the information that the library has acquired will have been wasted if users do not know how to contact the service or are unaware of the range of queries that could be answered by using it. In a small library it is likely that there will only be one point of contact for users and all queries will be directed through this source. This has the advantage for users of not having to anticipate who the best person to deal with their query would be and will allow the library to monitor responses and ensure consistency in how queries are handled, how answers are provided to users and how any deadlines set by the users are recorded. As part of developing this consistent approach you will also need to consider whether the library will limit its response to the simple provision of information or whether it will attempt to analyse or categorise the information found (for example, 'of the three sources found this one is the best').

Except for the more trivial examples, addresses or phone numbers for example, every enquiry should be recorded with details of how the enquiry was answered and how long it took to be answered. In any library common themes and questions will occur over a period of time and by recording the details of all enquiries patterns will emerge. Providing pre-prepared answers to such enquiries (though these answers will need to be checked from time to time to make sure that the answer is still relevant) is one way of managing the workload of the service as a whole and serves as a useful training tool for new staff.

The main difficulty with providing an enquiry service is that once established it needs to be able to deal effectively with all the enquiries it gets. Even when the library is located within an organisation with a very specialist nature, a bank for example, it will not always be possible to limit enquiries to the subject specialisation concerned. This has obvious implications for stock acquisition and emphasises again the need to build up a core collection of reference works to help meet this need. A list of useful general reference books is given in Appendix A.

Another difficulty that you may encounter is caused by users themselves not being sufficiently clear about what it is that they are looking for. In fact it is quite often the case that what you get asked for will only have the most superficial resemblance to the information required – you may be asked whether you have any books on statistics when what the user is looking for is very precise information about employment trends in a particular area. Part of the job of staff in the enquiry service will be to clarify what information the user wants. In librarianship this technique is often referred to as conducting the reference interview and a number of manuals detailing how this is done are given in the further reading section at the end of this chapter.

Inter-library loans

The question of inter-library loans and the extent to which libraries rely on them to supplement their own information holdings has been discussed already in Chapter 6 on stock. Rather than go over that ground again here we consider the service implications of providing a system for inter-library loans. There are a number of ways such a service could operate:

- *Through developing links with similar libraries locally.* This is an arrangement whereby libraries on a voluntary basis agree to loan material to one another subject to its availability. This can either be done on an ad hoc basis through personal contact (a group of law libraries or health-based library services, for example) or through a properly organised regional network. The London and Manchester Document Access service (LAMDA) which was set up to facilitate the exchange of serial articles between universities would be an example of this approach. In both instances arrangements can be made for the material to be delivered to your library.

- *Taking corporate membership of a larger library in the locality.* Some library services, particularly those in universities, allow other organisations to take out corporate membership of the library. This will normally take the form of issuing your library with a library card which will allow a certain number of items to be borrowed on it. Usually someone will have to go to the library to collect the individual items required.

- *Using one of the commercially available document delivery services.* There are a number of these which you could use ranging from OCLC First Search which gives access to more than 1.5 million full-text articles to the British Library Document Supply Service which handles nearly five million requests for documents every year.

The main difficulty with operating any system of inter-library loans, and particularly in the case of the various document supply centres, is trying to assess the impact of obtaining information this way on the library budget. If you do not know the extent of library usage under this heading then it is difficult to determine how much it will cost in any particular year. One way of trying to cope with the uncertainty is to fix a specific inter-library loans budget, although you will need to retain a degree of flexibility as you approach the end of the financial year. If you do borrow material from another library you need to ensure that you stick strictly to the terms on which it was loaned to you and have the necessary system in place to ensure that it can be returned at the appropriate time.

Current awareness

Current awareness services (or as they are sometimes called selective dissemination of information services) are the means by which the library informs its users about the latest publications and information. They can come in many different forms ranging from a simple list of titles recently acquired by the library to a more in-depth analysis of what is being published in particular subject areas. They also include such library staples as:

- photocopying the contents pages of selected journals;
- providing lists of journal articles;
- providing short abstracts of selected journal articles;
- newsletters informing users what the library is doing and providing information on new services;
- press cuttings services;
- subject guides.

Depending on the size of the library and number of regular users who would wish to use such a service, the amount of time and effort involved in operating such a service can be considerable. It entails creating user profiles for each of your users which attempts to match subject interest with information about what is currently being published or is about to be published in these subject areas. You will also need to decide how frequently your users will receive these updates, how you will communicate the details of the information to them and how much analysis of the information sources themselves you will include.

Current awareness services are certainly one way in which your users can be kept up to date about the latest developments in their particular field but as stated earlier they can be difficult to manage and do take up a great deal of staff time and effort. Before attempting to introduce such services you need to determine how important it is for your users to be kept up to date in this way and exactly what they want from the library.

Their views are extremely important. Do not assume that they will welcome your efforts here, or see current awareness as merely a marketing tool for the library, something that will raise library profile. It may do but not necessarily in the way that you expect. You do not want the library to have the reputation of being an organisation that does not help users manage information but only adds to the amount of information that needs managing. The sort of alerting service envisaged here is also provided by book suppliers and subscription agents as part of their value-added services and may be an option worth considering if you use either of these for the supply of books or serials.

One final point that needs to be considered in any discussion of operating current awareness services, particularly those which involve photocopying and circulating material direct from publishers (contents pages, for example) is to make sure that you comply with any copyright or licensing aspects which may be in operation. This is dealt with in Appendix B.

Training

One of the main ways of ensuring that your users get the maximum benefit from the library is to provide training for staff in all aspects of library provision. This means showing them how to use the catalogue and how to access the various library databases and CD-Roms that the library has purchased. Such training could also include sessions on the Internet, how to make best use of it and how to evaluate the information that is found there. You should also produce user guides for each of these products and make sure that they are always up to date and available in the library and over any internal networks which staff use. This training can be organised either on a one to one basis or through a number of open training sessions held throughout the year. Another way is to provide induction sessions for new staff. Most organisations have formal mechanisms for dealing with new entrants and it can be extremely useful if a 'how to use the library' session can be included in whatever induction arrangements are in place in your organisation.

Journal circulation

This has been considered previously in Chapter 6 on stock selection but a few words are appropriate here as this is a service that most specialist or technical libraries still carry out. Rather than purchase multiple copies of particular journals, due to the high costs involved, circulation lists are created for the journals that a number of users want to see on a regular basis and the journals are circulated to all those on the list in some specified order (either relating to when a particular person requested the journal or their seniority). Obviously these lists cannot be too long (a list with more than about five names on it will take too long to be read by everyone) and in any case they suffer from not being managed in any real sense by the library. (What happens to the circulation list if somebody on it is sick, on holiday or simply never gets round to passing it on?) The problem has been lessened to some extent with the advent of electronic journals but hard copy may still be the preferred format for many of your users.

Further reading

Corrall, Sheila (1994) *Strategic Planning for Library and Information Services*. Aslib.

Eckwright, Gail Z. (1994) *Reference Services Planning in the 90s*. Haworth Press.

Hamilton, Feona (1995) *Current Awareness, Current Techniques*. Ashgate.

Lobban, Margaret (2001) *Training Library Assistants*. Library Association Publishing.

Manual of Online Search Strategies (2001). Ashgate.

Parry, Julie (1995) *Induction*. Library Association Publishing.

Scammell, Alison (ed.) (2001) *Handbook of Information Management*. Taylor & Francis.

Webb, T.D. (2000) *Building Libraries for the 21st Century: The Shape of Information*. McFarland & Co.

Weingand, Darlene E. (1999) *Marketing and Planning Library and Information Services*. Greenwood Press.

8

Measuring the performance of the library service

At the beginning of our project we stressed the importance for the future development of the new library service of being in a position to show the management and staff within your organisation the benefits that starting the new service would bring. In this chapter we consider the sort of evidence that you might need in order to show that those benefits have been realised and the range of performance measures that is needed to support this. In any event it is always important for a library manager to try and evaluate how things are going and to see if the targets you have set yourself have been met. In today's climate of accountability this is something that you are likely to have to do on a continuous basis so you need to be prepared in advance to be able to deal with any queries asked of you. Performance measures, in this sense, are no more than management tools which will help you to find out how well your service is performing and draw attention to those areas that need looking at in order for improvements to be made.

However, for a library, this is not a particularly easy task. Performance measurement in a service which is predominantly about people must be more than just data collection, although data collection will be a part of it. As we have seen in the chapter dealing with stock selection it is not always easy to determine the effectiveness of the services you are providing. Adopting performance measures will help but no matter how detailed they are, they will never be anything other than indicators of how well or how badly things are going. They may provide evidence but that evidence will need to be carefully considered before any decisions are taken as a result. Careful judgement will be required which must be based on a thorough knowledge of why the data was being collected in the first place, what the exact nature of the evidence it produces is, and how it relates to the needs and expectations of library users.

The reasons why measuring performance is important

Part of the process of developing a new library service has been to show how the library can become a valuable asset for its parent organisation. In order to do this, libraries must be able to demonstrate their value in ways which are simple to understand and which can be measured in a quantitative way. In Chapter 1 we discussed how crucial information was for organisations to function effectively and the problems they encountered when information was not managed properly. We also discussed the role that libraries could play in this process and used the arguments we developed to show how they could be used in building the case for creating new library services. As the library grows the use of performance measures will serve to reinforce these arguments and to provide hard evidence to underpin continued support and investment for the library. Unless the library can prove its worth in terms of the effectiveness, cost-effectiveness and efficiency of the services it provides and how the existence of these services benefit the organisation as a whole it is unlikely to have a viable future.

This is particularly the case in situations where there is competition for resources or where resources are being reduced at all levels within the parent organisation. Except in very unusual circumstances libraries do not contribute directly to the business functions of organisations but support them in indirect ways (by providing access to external sources of information that the organisation needs and by managing that information effectively). This means that the library must be able to quantify the importance of this function and show how useful, relevant and valuable this support is, how it relates to the business needs of the organisation, and how much the organisation would perform less effectively if the library was not there. In this situation the main purpose of performance measures is to illustrate the benefits of providing resources to the library so that the library can persuade senior managers within the organisation to continue providing them.

So far we have discussed performance measurement simply in terms of how the library relates to its parent organisation. While this is extremely important, performance measurement can also be used to support decisions that librarians have to make for operational reasons to manage their service more effectively. Librarians need to make decisions all the time. To do this properly they need some basic information on which to base these decisions. The use of performance measures in areas such as:

- the allocation of resources
- target setting
- stock selection
- planning and developing new services
- determining priorities

will allow these management processes to operate in a situation grounded in a sound knowledge of what is actually going on. The use of effective performance measures will enable you, for example, to:

- understand how the library is performing against the objectives that you have set;
- compare how performance changes from one year to the next and from one site to another if you are operating on a multi-site basis;
- consider the benefits of existing services in terms of the resources allocated to them;
- decide about the future resourcing of particular services;
- determine the effects of either reducing or increasing resources in particular areas;
- check that all library activities are continuing to support the basic objectives of the parent organisation as a whole.

Performance measurement does this in terms of providing evidence in the form of data to answer a number of basic questions that should be considered in the context of overall library management. These questions can be summarised as follows:

- How far is the library meeting its strategic objectives?
- How well is the library meeting the business needs of the parent organisation?
- How well are library resources being allocated?
- Is the balance between expenditure on stock and expenditure on services the correct one?
- Is the balance between expenditure on electronic resources and printed information correct?
- Is the balance between expenditure on serial publications and monographs correct?
- How well is the library satisfying user needs and meeting user expectations?
- What percentage of potential users are actually using the library?
- Do library opening hours reflect the expectations of library users?
- Has the overall performance of the library improved in a consistent manner over previous years?

As stated earlier, these questions need to be considered in the context of a general management process. This cannot be emphasised strongly enough. Whatever system of performance measurement is adopted this point must not be overlooked. One of the problems of collecting data of any sort is that sometimes the hard work involved in collecting it can distort the management process so that the act of collection itself becomes the main purpose of the exercise. Data is then collected because it always has been and statistical information is maintained, on books borrowed to take a simple example, because that is what the library does. If this becomes the case then it will be difficult, if not impossible, to identify exactly what the performance measures were meant to show and what positive action the library should be taking as a result. The context in which the development of a system of performance measurement should be grounded is one that you should be familiar with from previous chapters but it is worth repeating here one more time. In order to successfully promote the use of performance measurement for your library you need to consider the following:

- the precise nature of your library operation;
- what the main purpose of the library is;
- how the library supports the business needs of its parent organisation;
- what objectives have been set for the library;
- what targets are in place;
- what is likely to prevent you from fulfilling those objectives and meeting those targets;
- how you will judge success;
- how others will judge it;
- what the exact nature of your customer base is;
- what services are in place to meet their needs.

In answering these questions you will be able to determine the areas in which you need to develop supporting evidence in order to judge whether or not the library is being successful. From this you can then construct the measures which will be most useful in providing you with the evidence you require.

Inputs, outputs and outcomes

Performance measurement in libraries is usually discussed in terms of inputs, outputs and outcomes where:

- inputs are the resources which are deployed within the library in terms of staff, accommodation, physical material including stock and so on;
- outputs are the sum of the total library operation, what it does and what it produces as a result (the number of items added to stock, the number of information queries answered, the number of items loaned to users);
- outcomes are the use made by customers of the library and how satisfied they were with the quality of the service they received and the quality of the manner in which they received it.

While it is relatively easy to measure both inputs and outputs as these are essentially known elements completely under the control of the library, it is much more difficult to assess outcomes in a satisfactory way. Customer satisfaction can be measured by surveys, for example, though there is a limit to the number of surveys that users can be expected to respond to in a given period.

What is really difficult to assess, however, is the impact that access to library services has on individuals who use it and subsequently on the organisation itself. Yet the library may be required to show how it has contributed to, for example:

- the overall effectiveness and efficiency of the parent organisation;
- the profitability of the parent organisation;
- the overall delivery of the parent organisation's aims and objectives;
- the development of staff.

It may be relatively easy to show that by creating a library service the organisation has managed to reduce the amount of money spent on the acquisition of books and journals and access to electronic sources of information, but this is not quite the same thing as it could be argued that even more could have been saved if none of these things had been purchased in the first place. And yet some attempt must be made to show how the library has contributed to the overall well-being of the organisation if arguments for the continued funding of the library are to be successful.

However, before considering this further, a number of general points about performance measurement need to be made. Whatever performance measurement system is put in place a single set of measurements will not be enough. Measurement needs to take place over a number of years so that comparisons can be made and trends identified, either of improvement in service delivery or of deterioration. Measurement needs to be consistent, so that figures are collected in the same way over time or adjustments are made to take account of any enforced variation. To be of use as aids in taking decisions they also need to conform to the following set of principles which are based on those previously identified by Ford in his article on 'Approaches to performance measurement'.[1] They must:

- be relevant to the area of service being analysed;
- be helpful in highlighting potential problem areas and drawing attention to areas of concern;
- actually measure what they were designed to measure and not something else;
- be reliable and consistent over time;
- be accurate;
- be practical in the sense that the effort involved in collecting the data appropriate to the measure should not outweigh the potential benefits of collecting it.

Of these, the last which we looked at earlier in considering the place of performance management in the context of overall library management is obviously the most important. For performance measurement to work properly you need to have a clear understanding of what you want to achieve and to know exactly the reasons for collecting data in the first place. There will be a significant difference, for example, between data which is being collected as part of a reporting mechanism to senior management and data which is being collected as part of an internal assessment of how to improve services both in the detail of the type of data being collected and in the way it is presented.

The actual act of data collection may require significant time and effort so that while any number of performance measures could be put in place, you need to consider carefully the effort involved and how this can be integrated with the work you and other library staff are already carrying out. It may be better to concentrate on only a few measures that can be fitted into existing working patterns and arrangements so that you can remain committed to them over time as this is essential if the data that you collect is to have real value. What is important is not necessarily the actual figures that you collect but how they change over time so that you can compare library performance from one year to the next.

By integrating performance measurement work into your overall library plan you will be able to decide the areas which are important for you to monitor and against which the service will be judged and then select the most appropriate measures. Performance measurement can take many forms from the simple to the complex. Routine library work, for example, could be measured in terms of:

- the number of registered library users;
- the number of items added to stock;
- the number of items borrowed;
- the number of information requests completed;
- the number of library users over a particular period.

Data like this will then allow a number of effectiveness and efficiency measures to be calculated based on the overall cost of providing the library service or the number of staff engaged in each pursuit, the unit cost of borrowing a library book, the cost per member of staff, the unit cost of answering an information request and so on. You will need to decide for yourself how useful such figures are likely to be either for you as a library manager or for management in the wider organisation.

Again, depending on the nature of your library, performance measurement could also take the following forms:

- *The number of regular users of the library service as a percentage of the number of staff entitled to use the library.* This will indicate how relevant the library is seen to be to the organisation as a whole and will show how far the library has penetrated its potential market.

- *The satisfaction of users with the service being provided.* This will indicate how users are responding both to how the library is performing and to the range of services being provided (although you should be warned that it is not always easy to get reliable responses from those you work closely with).

- *The total time spent on responding to information enquiries and the percentage of them answered effectively within 24 hours, within 2–3 days, within a week and so on.* This will indicate the complexity of the information enquiries being dealt with and the efficiency with which they are being handled. (If new material needs to be acquired in order for some of the enquiries to be answered satisfactorily this measurement will also contribute to an analysis of collection development and on the speed of processing material for users.)

- *The number of user induction sessions that the library puts on.* This is another way of gauging market penetration and finding out about the services that users find most useful.

■ *The use made of any current awareness services being provided by the library.* In this area the views of non-users of the service will be as valid as those of users (why they don't use the service, what changes could be made that would encourage them to become users and so on).

This type of performance measurement, as well as providing quantitative evidence, will also allow you to make a qualitative judgement about how well the library is performing and the impact that the provision of library services is having on both users and the organisation.

As stated earlier the majority of performance indicators will only measure inputs and outputs, and while measurement here can be of use in helping to monitor library performance and to enable you to respond to changing situations, they will not measure the actual value of the library or the way in which the library contributes to the success of the parent organisation by helping it improve or become more efficient. There is no easy way to do this. The only satisfactory way that this can be done is for the people who have used the service to tell you how the information they obtained from the library or was obtained for them by a member of the library staff was crucial for the success of a project or helped them achieve a specific goal or target. This is why the involvement of users in developing the library service in the first place was so crucial and why the need to consult widely with users for all aspects of service development was emphasised so strongly in earlier chapters.

The work of the library needs to be totally integrated with the work of the organisation as a whole, with the library at the centre of things rather than on the periphery. This means knowing exactly what your parent organisation is doing at all times, what is important for it, how its priorities have changed and what new aspects of work are being developed, and then designing a library service that takes this work as its core concern and develops library services around it.

Developing a system for performance measurement

Having decided on the sorts of performance measures that you wish to introduce you now need to develop a system that will allow you to collect the data you need without interfering with ongoing library work. The most important aspect of developing this system is to ensure that the processes involved are seen as being part of the normal processes of management. This will ensure that the tasks involved in collecting the required data are incorporated into working patterns and are not seen as something outside the normal flow of work. How this will be done will, to a large extent, be dictated by the work situation, how many staff you have and what their responsibilities are, but you will certainly need to consider some of the following before you begin:

- *The strategic purpose of any measurement activity* – what you want to measure, who the measurement is for and what you hope to achieve by it.

- *Who will be involved in the measurement process* – do they understand what the measurement is for and have they received the appropriate training to do what they are supposed to do.

- *How the data will be collected* – on an ongoing basis or at some specified time. (Depending on the information being collected it may be better to devote a specific period to it rather than try to analyse every occurrence. If you are attempting to measure the time taken to handle information queries, for example, it will not be practical to try and do this for every enquiry. It might be better to set aside certain weeks throughout the year, say four periods of five days, and then extrapolate your findings here to a full year. If you do this, however, you need to make sure that the periods chosen do not all occur when the library is busiest but are representative of library activity throughout the year.)

- *How the data will be analysed* – particularly if you are using representative samples.

- *How the data that is collected can inform the decision-making process of the library* – there is no point in collecting data for the sake of it. Any information that you collect should have a purpose otherwise it will simply become a distraction from the real work that the library needs to do.

Having done this you should now know what data you need to collect and how you are going to collect it. This will provide the basis for the further development of the system and its integration into the overall work of the service.

While quite a lot of the data that you collect will be either system generated (the number of library users, the amount of library stock) or collected by library staff (the time spent on information queries, the number of users attending library induction sessions) much of the information that you need can only be obtained from the users themselves. This is where you will generate the most interesting information about the outcomes of the services offered and the impact they have had on overall business performance. You should remember, however, that while it may be extremely important for the library to collect such information it may not always suit your users to give it, for reasons that are entirely understandable. Whether you decide to garner this information through user satisfaction questionnaires, interviews or group discussions, the convenience of users remains paramount. You should not ask them to participate in these activities more than they are willing to do so nor ask them over and over again how they think the library is performing!

You will already have expended considerable energy in trying to build up relationships with users and you should try not to impose too often on the willingness of users to be helpful and considerate. This particular interaction needs careful thought if you are not to undermine good working relations and you should be careful to minimise the time that users can expect to be involved with this sort of consultation by:

- only asking questions which are capable of being answered;
- only asking what it is essential to know, not what would be nice to know;

- only asking those questions which can be realistically (and truthfully) answered;
- only asking those questions which users will be prepared to answer;
- only asking for information which is unobtainable by any other means.[2]

By restricting your questions in this way to the areas which are of vital concern to the library and essential for the further development of the service, and by making the exercise as painless as possible for the users concerned, you will not damage the hard-won advantage that you will have gained by involving users at every stage of the project.

If handled properly, the introduction of a formal system of performance measurement and a proper emphasis on taking account of the views of users can be of great assistance with the process of library development. It can be useful by helping to define objectives and by sharpening up the management of target setting. At the same time it will also help create a more formal basis for involving users in service development. It will, however, always need to be more than the simple collection of data. Libraries are first and foremost about service to people and if performance measurement is not fundamentally about ways in which these services can be improved continuously then they will never meet the objectives you have set for them.

Notes

1. G. Ford (1989) 'Approaches to performance measurement: some observations on principles and practice', *British Journal of Academic Librarianship*, 4(2), 74–87.

2. King Research Ltd (1990) *Keys to Success: Performance Indicators for Public Libraries*. Office of Arts and Libraries.

Further reading

Abbot, Christine (1994) *Performance Measurement in Library and Information Services*. Aslib.

Brophy, Peter and Couling, Kate (1996) *Quality Management for Information and Library Managers*. Ashgate.

Harbour, Jerry L. (1997) *Basics of Performance Measurement*. Quality Resources.

Jordan, Peter and Lloyd, Carline (2002) *Staff Management in Library and Information Work*, 4th edn. Ashgate.

Orr, R.H. (1993) 'Measuring the goodness of library services: a general framework for considering quantitative measures', *Journal of Documentation*, 29, 315–32.

9

Marketing the new service

By this stage of the project we have gone a long way towards identifying the basic shape and confines of the new service. We have identified who the customers are, collected together, classified and catalogued the library material already in the possession of the organisation and planned how the service will be delivered. In considering service development further we now need to engage customers more fully in the process so that they can be better informed about what the library does and how it will meet customer expectation. This can be done through marketing; the development of a marketing plan will help you focus the strategic goals you have set for the library in ways which will complement the activities of your organisation and help it achieve its aims and objectives.

Marketing is about a state of mind as much as anything else and plans do not need to be too sophisticated or grandiose to be successful. In a sense its basic aim is to provide a focus for the things you do that is firmly centred on customers and customer need. The process itself is fairly straightforward. To begin, you will need to have:

- a clear understanding of what you want to achieve with the library service and the activities that you consider crucial for success;

- a thorough knowledge of your organisation's overall aims and objectives and how the library can be positioned to help in their achievement;

- an ability to communicate effectively with staff at all levels in the organisation;

- an ability to interpret and present information in a variety of ways;

- the enthusiasm and commitment to overcome problems and difficulties in dealing with people who may not see the relevance for them of what you are trying to achieve.

In Chapter 3 we discussed the importance of creating a customer-based service and marketing can be seen as one way of ensuring that you do not lose sight of this objective as the library service develops. In this sense marketing is the process by which the librarian identifies, anticipates and satisfies customer needs in ways which best meet the customer's requirements both as they exist now and how they might appear in the future.

As such, the marketing plan as a process needs to consider the full range of library activities and determine how best they can be fitted within the overall context of the library's operational plan. These activities will include:

- finding out who the library's customers are and the nature of their current and future needs;

- analysing how the library can be organised to meet that need in the most effective and appropriate ways;

- looking at what strengths and weaknesses that the library has that will either help or hinder the process;

- developing appropriate services and products to meet customer need as a result of this analysis; and finally

- monitoring and measuring how these services and products actually fulfil their function and what your customers think of them.

As you will probably have recognised, many of these activities are the same as those that have already been discussed earlier. The concept of marketing and the development of marketing plans puts these activities and their customer orientation firmly at the centre of library thinking: by emphasising the fact that these activities are not to be undertaken on a one-off basis but must underpin the whole operation of the library and the context in which things are done. As we have already seen, customers and their needs change and the library must act in a dynamic way to meet the challenge of this change to stay successful.

Identifying customers

In looking at customers in this way there are a number of key questions which must be answered. Some of these you will have already considered but it is useful to look at them again in the context of developing your marketing plan. Even if you think you already have the answers to the questions it is worth considering them once more. You may be surprised at some of the information that the process throws up. The key questions are:

- Who are your customers?
- Where are they situated within the organisation and what do they do?
- What are they like as individuals and what are the essential characteristics of the work they do?
- What are their general requirements for information?
- What are their specific requirements?
- Why do they use the library?
- What services do they find most beneficial at the moment?
- What services do they not use at the moment?
- How will this change in the future?
- What do you need to do to persuade them to keep using the library or to use the library more?

The answers to these questions will enable you to do a number of things. You will learn why your customers value the library service and what they think of the range of services on offer. You will begin to understand their needs and expectations and this information will enable you to concentrate your efforts in areas which are the most appropriate for you to develop in order to improve services in line with those needs and expectations. It will also help you in deciding how to best inform your customers of what you are doing and what changes you are introducing.

While it is certainly true that all customers are different and that, as a result, their needs will also be different and will vary over time, it is still possible to group them together for the purposes of marketing in terms of who they are, what they do and the position they occupy in the organisation. Depending on the nature of your organisation, it is likely to consist of some or all of the following types of staff:

- senior managers
- legal staff
- administrative staff
- statisticians
- researchers
- sales staff
- maintenance workers

and so on. These in turn can be further classified by:

- age
- information handling skills
- information need
- knowledge
- experience
- extent to which they are likely to use the library.

Combining the two sets of results will provide a reasonable approximation of the make-up of staff in your organisation. You should then test this picture against your own experience and the experience of other library staff to make it as complete as possible. By doing this you will easily be able to identify the areas in which to concentrate your initial marketing efforts in order to maximise the resources you have at your disposal. You should now be in a position that will enable you to:

- determine which customers are most likely to respond enthusiastically to the work you are doing;
- identify the services which will be most useful to them;
- focus your efforts in those areas where you are most likely to succeed;
- recognise quickly potential changes within the organisation;
- design and direct promotional activities which are best suited to the needs of these core customers.

However, in order to do this successfully you must not only have a thorough understanding of your customer base but also develop a complete picture of how your organisation operates – what it does, the business segment it operates in, the factors and legislation that govern and limit its activities. This in turn will then influence the information that your customers will need in order for them to work in this environment and to carry out their various roles and responsibilities within it. This knowledge will enable you to satisfy current need and, perhaps more importantly, allow you to anticipate what those needs will be in the future and how they might change.

Developing a marketing strategy

Having undertaken this preliminary work you will now be in a position to start developing you marketing strategy. Marketing is a business process and shares a common approach with many other similar processes. In order to be effective it needs to be grounded in the particular circumstances of your own organisation. This means that you need to develop a programme that will assist you in:

- understanding the business objectives of the organisation as a whole;
- setting objectives for the library which detail how the library will assist the organisation achieve those objectives;
- devising a strategy which will detail how the library objectives are to be met;
- planning how the strategy will be delivered;
- setting goals and targets to measure performance against the plan;
- revising and revisiting the objectives on a continuous basis to ensure that your strategy is working and to make whatever changes are needed to keep the momentum of the plan going.

In terms of marketing in the traditional sense this will mean producing an action plan which concentrates on the following elements, often known as the 4 'Ps':

- *product* – services designed to meet the customers' needs;
- *price* – reflecting the cost of the resources needed to supply the service;
- *place* – the manner in which the services are made available to customers;
- *promotion* – the ways in which customers are made aware of the services on offer.

A fifth 'P' – people (meaning those who will be delivering the service) – is sometimes also included but is excluded here: because, as you are likely either to be working on your own or operating with only a small team, it is assumed that marketing the library service will be an integral part of the whole team's responsibilities.

This particular model has its origins in the consumer goods sector where what is being produced and marketed are actual products. It can still be usefully applied, however, when considering the marketing of library services, provided you have an understanding of the differences between providing services and providing products. These differences are usually discussed in terms of:

- *intangibility* – the difficulty in defining exactly what 'product' is being provided;

- *inseparability* – the difficulty in distinguishing between the service and the service provider;

- *consistency* – the difficulty in ensuring that the level of service being provided is the same no matter what member of staff carries out the actual work;

- *shelf life* – the fact that service 'products' are related to particular circumstances and cannot be stored away for later use.

But if these factors are taken into account then the basic structure of the 4 'Ps' can still be adapted to form the framework for your marketing plan. This works in the following way:

- *Product* – the service you are offering: the books, journals and electronic databases that you have, the way they are arranged and the ways in which you use them to meet the information needs of your users.

- *Price* – the resources that the library consumes in terms of staff, equipment, buildings and stock acquisition in providing its service whether or not this cost is passed on to users in accounting terms.

- *Place* – the physical location of the library together with the manner in which services are made available to users, through information networks, mail or telephone.

- *Promotion* – the way in which the library tells users what it actually does and how the benefits and value of the service is communicated.

Communicating the message

Again there should be nothing surprising in any of this. In essence, marketing is really only an extension of the customer-based approach that we discussed in Chapter 3. Every point of contact between the library and its users can be defined in terms of the marketing process and every interaction is a marketing opportunity. What the marketing plan does is to establish a link between library users and the services that the library is offering in a formal way so that the services can be analysed and measured. It means putting together a plan which states explicitly how the library operates and what it wants to achieve for its customers. The marketing plan also becomes the mechanism by which the library:

- finds out why existing customers use the service, what benefits it brings and how services could be improved;
- finds out why potential customers go elsewhere and establishing what the library can do to change this;
- finds out about the negative as well as the positive images of the library.

This in turn will enable the library to adapt and change the way it does things as a consequence in order to meet needs that have not previously been anticipated and ensure that customer focus remains at the heart of everything the library does.

How you put the plan into operation depends on the nature of the organisation you work for, how its internal communication systems work and the style of management in current operation. Approaches can either be formal or informal, either through friendly chats or more structured formal presentations. It can encompass a range of material from posters to library bookmarks, mouse mats to suggested reading lists, articles in in-house magazines to specially produced library newsletters, depending on the budget and how customers will welcome any of the above. You will know yourself how your organisation likes to work and which of the above, either singly or in combination, will work for you. You will also know what you and your staff are good at and will feel most comfortable doing. If one method does not work try another until you get one that does. Be imaginative and above all enthusiastic. Whatever the format the purpose remains the same and so will have the same functions, namely:

- creating awareness of the library's existence;
- listing what the library does and how it does it;
- creating the impression that the library and its staff are friendly and have the necessary professional expertise to be able to help users find the information that they want;
- promoting the library as an important asset for the organisation;
- reminding users that if they do not need these services immediately the library will be there when they do.

Remember too that the library itself is an important asset to be used as part of the marketing plan. You should try to make it as welcome and open as possible as this will influence how customers react to the services on offer and the way in which you and your staff carry them out. Obviously this will depend on the budget allocated to the library and on the office space you have been given – but as far as possible the library should be there for the convenience of customers, not staff. Thus it should be:

- open hours that suit the way customers work;
- convenient to where the majority of staff work;
- welcoming in terms of arrangement and lighting with adequate study space if required and separate areas for newspapers and magazines;

- well-guided with shelf guides up to date and in the right places;

- staffed by appropriately skilled library personnel accessible to customers at all times.

A few last words on marketing

As I have already stated, the concept of marketing works best when it is considered as an extension of developing services based on customer need. In this light it can be seen to be appropriate in all library situations and necessary for all types of library. It is really the process of trying to find the best match between what the library does and what customers expect it should do, and communicating that message to those customers. Like all processes it requires hard work and imagination but if your library does not attract and then retain sufficient satisfied customers it will not survive, no matter what innovative services are on offer or how good the library is at delivering them. As consumers, library users behave no differently than they do in other situations. They expect the widest possible choice. They insist that their demands are met immediately. They demand easy access to a whole range of information products and services. Marketing is the management process which will enable you to differentiate your services from all other potential rivals in a way that will help you to concentrate your skills and expertise on developing the products and services that your customers require now and in the future.

Further reading

Coote, Helen (1994) *How to Market Your Library Service Effectively*. Aslib.

Cronin, Blaise (1992) *The Marketing of Library and Information Services*. Aslib.

de Elliott, Eileen (2002) *Marketing Concepts for Libraries and Information Services*. Saez.

Rowley, Jennifer (2001) *Information Marketing*. Ashgate.

Walters, Suzanne (2003) *Library Marketing that Works*. Neal-Schuman Publishers.

Weingand, Darlene E. (1999) *Marketing and Planning Library and Information Services*. Greenwood Press.

10

Conclusion

We have now reached the end of the project. However, that does not mean that our work has ended. Before considering this point further it is worth looking back on what we have achieved so far and enumerate the main lessons we have learned.

In a very real sense, through creating a new library service, we have been able to create order out of chaos and by bringing better discipline to the management of information within our organisation, and contributed to an overall improvement in business efficiency. We have done this by:

- bringing together the disparate information resources of the organisation;
- arranging those resources to improve access and retrieval;
- identifying gaps in information provision and improving the range and quality of available information;
- developing new services to meet information need;
- promoting the use of the information sources to ensure improved value for money;
- measuring how the information sources are used and setting targets for improvement.

All of this has been achieved by hard work and by putting the needs and concerns of library users at the heart of everything we do. This last point cannot be emphasised too strongly nor repeated too often. Libraries are first and foremost about people, about the information they need and the ways in which they gain access to it and use it. This fact needs to be absorbed by all library staff and every effort made to ensure that continued library development retains it as its governing principle. This will not always be easy to do. As every organisation evolves it develops its own momentum for change, based on how it did things in the past and the internal dynamic that grows up between existing members of staff. In this way, internal processes can evolve which suit the convenience of library staff rather than benefit library users. You will need to guard against this as your library matures by looking continuously at ways to improve communication between your library and its users and by finding ways to involve them as the library continues to change and develop.

It is because libraries are so grounded in the needs of individuals that the work to establish a new library service can be said to be always incomplete. As we saw in an earlier chapter, life in a library does not stay still. Individual needs change as people change jobs or are given new responsibilities. New staff will be taken on and even if the essentials of their jobs remain the same as those of the people they replace, their individual information needs will not be the same nor will their expectation of how the library service will meet them. At the same time the nature of information itself is also always changing as new products are developed and new technologies emerge which change the ways in which information is processed and delivered.

This is the environment in which you will be working as a librarian and in order to succeed you will need to be able to react flexibly to the changes you will inevitably face. This means that your library service itself will have to have a built in flexibility that will allow you to respond to change quickly and find new and innovative ways of meeting the changing needs of users.

I hope you have found this short guide useful. I said at the beginning that the task of creating and maintaining a new library service would be a difficult and challenging one, even more so if you are operating on your own. However, despite the inherent difficulties, the job of making links between library users and the information that they need is a particularly rewarding one. Augustine Birrell had it exactly right when he said that 'libraries are not made, they grow'.[1] I hope that you have years of fun growing yours.

Note

1. Sourced from IFLANET, the website of the International Federation of Library Associations and Institutions (*http://www.ifla.org/I/humour/subj.htm#coll*).

Appendix A
Useful reference publications

The following is a list of some of the most useful multi-purpose reference sources that should be included in any library. They are broken down into broad subject areas. The list does not include dictionaries or thesauri but these should also be included as part of your reference collection.

Comprehensive facts and figures

- *Whitaker's Almanac*. J. Whitaker & Sons
- *Statesman's Yearbook: The Politics, Cultures and Economies of the World*. Palgrave Macmillan
- *Britain: The Official Yearbook of the United Kingdom*. Stationery Office.

People

- *International Who's Who*. Europa Publications
- *Who's Who*. Europa Publications

Events and dates

- D.S. Lewis and Aileen Harvey, *The Annual Register: A Record of World Events*. Keesings Worldwide

Statistics

- *Annual Abstract of Statistics*. The Stationery Office
- *Regional Trends*. The Stationery Office
- *Social Trends*. The Stationery Office
- *Eurostat Yearbook: The Statistical Guide to Europe*. Eurostat
- *Statistical Yearbook*. United Nations Publications
- *World Marketing Data and Statistics*. Euromonitor

Associations and organisations

- *Directory of British Associations and Associations in Ireland*. CBD Research
- *Aslib Directory of Information Sources in the United Kingdom*. Aslib
- *Hollis UK Press and Public Relations Annual*. Hollis Publishing
- *Europa Directory of International Organizations*. Europa Publications
- *Yearbook of International Organizations*. Gale Group

Periodicals

- *Willing's Press Guide.* Waymaker
- *Benn's Media.* CMP International
- *Ulrich's International Periodicals Directory.* Bowker Press

There are a number of books currently available which will be of assistance in developing the sort of quick-reference enquiry service in which these titles would be used. A good starting point would be:

- Tim Owen (2000) *Success at the Enquiry Desk*, 3rd edn. Library Association Publishing

Appendix B
Copyright

The question of copyright is a difficult one for librarians but it is something which must be considered as it affects much of the work that they do. This book is not really the appropriate place to consider the question in any detail, not least because I am not a lawyer. I reproduce below some initial guidance produced by the Government Library Service in Northern Ireland as part of library induction training for new staff. While not a complete treatise on copyright by any means, it is a useful introduction to the subject.

What is copyright?

Copyright gives legal protection to the creators of certain kinds of material so that they can control the way their work may be exploited. There is no official register for copyright and, as such, there is no official action to take, for example applying for copyright status or registration. The types of works that copyright protects are:

■ original literary works, for example novels, instruction manuals, computer programs and song lyrics;

- original dramatic works, including works of dance or mime;
- original musical works;
- original artistic works, for example paintings and photographs;
- published editions of works, that is the typographical arrangement of a publication;
- sound recordings on any medium;
- films;
- broadcasts and cable programmes.

These works are protected by copyright, regardless of the medium in which they exist and this includes the Internet. This is also the case if the work has not actually been published. However, copyright does not protect ideas. It protects the way the idea is expressed in a piece of work, not the idea itself.

Duration of copyright

In general a work is in copyright for 70 years after the death of the author, or 70 years from when the work was first made available to the public. However, every published work has two copyrights: one in the actual content of the text (the author's creative work, where copyright exists for 70 years after the author's death) and the other in the printed layout of the page (the publisher's typography, where copyright exists for 25 years). Special rules apply to Crown and Parliamentary materials.

Libraries and copying

In simple terms what copyright is intended to do is to protect the creative output of individuals from general use without their permission. No work can be protected by copyright if it is not original and copyright will not have been infringed unless a substantial part of it is copied. In the UK there is a general right to copy, called fair dealing, which allows copying to be carried out under specific, limited circumstances. This can only be applied for the specific purposes of research and private study, criticism or review, and news reporting (of text not photographs). Under this fair dealing provision, libraries can provide copies of original works to users under the following conditions:

- only one copy of the required information is made;
- it is intended to be used for one of the purposes listed above;
- the user signs a form confirming that the purpose of copying is covered by one of the purposes listed above;
- the copy has not previously been supplied by the library;
- the library retains the form.

While there is no legal definition of what 'substantial' means in this context, past practice would indicate that you should not exceed the following limits:

- one complete chapter from a published work or 5 per cent of the text taken as extracts;

- no more than one article from a serial publication in any one issue. (Interestingly, in UK law an article is defined as 'an item of any description' and as a result includes contents and title pages, indexes, letters to the editor, advertisements as well what are usually thought of as articles.)

In addition:

- illustrations can only be copied as part of an extract or periodical article, not on their own;
- digitised works must be for your own personal use and must not be stored, circulated to other people or published on a network.

Of course anything can be copied if you have the rights holder's permission. Some of these rights holders do give blanket permission for some copying to take place. Examples of this include:

- 10 per cent from a British Standard;
- unrestricted copying from Lords and Commons Official Reports and other parliamentary papers provided that no more than one copy is made for any individual and that copies are not further distributed;
- certain crown copyright material including legislation and government press notices.

Best practice

If you have any doubts about a particular request for copying you should always err on the side of caution and contact the author, usually via the publisher, for permission to copy. For general copyright queries the British Library Copyright Office is a good place to start. They can be contacted at: *http://www .bl.uk/services/informtion/copyright.html.*

It is also possible to obtain a licence which will greatly extend the scope of copying that can be done by a library without seeking further permission. Information on licences in the UK can be obtained by contacting the Copyright Licensing Agency at: *http://www.cla.co.uk/.*

Further reading

Cornish, Graham (1997) 'Copyright', in *Handbook of Special Librarianship and Information Work*, 7th edn. Aslib.

Gurnsey, John (1994) *Copyright Theft*. Ashgate.

Minow, Mary and Lipinski, Thomas A. (2002) *The Library's Legal Answer Book*. American Library Association.

Pedley, Paul (2000) *Copyright for Library and Information Service Professionals*, 2nd edn. Aslib.

Index

access model, 78
access points, 54, 65
acquisition policies, 76–9
Anglo-American Cataloguing
    Rules, 62–6

British Library Document Supply
    Centre, 111
British National Bibliography, 58
budgets, 73–6, 111

cataloguing, 53–68
cataloguing rules, 62–6
circulation, 105–6
classification, 31–52
classification schemes, 40–9
classifying information, 50–1
collection development policies,
    76–9
computerised cataloguing, 54–5,
    66–8
copyright, 157–61
current awareness, 111–13
customer-based services, 139–40

Dewey Decimal Classification,
    42–5
disposal, 32
document supply, 78

electronic information 84–7
electronic serials, 88–91
enumerative cataloguing, 38,
    45–7, 48

faceted classification, 39, 48
finding lists, 56

general classification schemes,
    42–7
getting started, 9–18
GMDs, 58

information:
    as an asset, 3, 11–13
    as a resource, 1
information age, 2
information audit, 12–13, 22, 31,
    72–4, 84
information management, 3–5
information retrieval, 33, 36, 54
information society, 2
inputs, 123–6
inter-library loans, 77–8, 110–11
Internet, 23, 91–7
ISBN, 58

journal circulation, 84, 114
journals, 31

keywords, 55–6

library cooperation, 3
library management systems, 58,
    66–8, 106
Library of Congress Classification
    Scheme, 45–7, 58
library users, 15, 18, 21–9, 33, 51

MARC records, 57–8
marketing, 135–47
marketing strategy, 140–3
monographs, 79–82
Moys Classification Scheme, 48–9

notation, 38–40, 41

OCLC First Search, 111
OPACs, 55, 66
outcomes, 123–9
outputs, 123–9

performance measurement, 74,
    117–32
planning, 99–104
precision, 62
preparation, 9–11

quick reference material, 153–5

recall, 62
reference material, 153–5
reference interview, 109
role of librarian, 5–6

selective dissemination of
    information, 111
serials, 82–5
service development, 24, 28,
    99–114
shelf marks, 56
specialist classification schemes,
    47–9
stock selection, 71–97
subscriptions, 90–1

training 113–14

user needs, 25–8, 34, 53, 55, 76,
    86–7, 100, 128, 149

value of information, 1–2
virtual libraries, 78